Between Auschwitz
and Tradition

VALUE INQUIRY BOOK SERIES

VIBS

Volume 6

Robert Ginsberg
Executive Editor

Associate Editors

a volume in
Holocaust and Genocide Studies
HGS

Alan Rosenberg and Alan Milchman, Editors

Between Auschwitz and Tradition

postmodern reflections on the task of thinking

James R. Watson

photographs by the author

To Alan M,
who understands
America the Beautiful
and its many codes.
Thank you for everything.
Jim Watson

Rodopi

Amsterdam - Atlanta, GA 1994

Cover design by Chris Kok based on a photograph, ©1984 by Robert
Ginsberg, of statuary by Gustav Vigeland in the Frogner Park, Oslo,
Norway.

ISBN: 90-5183-567-1 (CIP)
©Editions Rodopi B.V., Amsterdam - Atlanta, GA 1994
Printed in The Netherlands

To Suzette, who shares all of this.

Contents

list of photographs

Page	Title	Location

editorial foreword

The appearance of James R. Watson's *Between Auschwitz and Tradition: Postmodern Reflections on the Task of Thinking*, as the first volume in a special series, Holocaust and Genocide Studies (HGS) within the Value Inquiry Book Series (VIBS), necessitates some comment on both the book itself, and on the special series which it launches. This is all the more the case inasmuch as Watson's *Between Auschwitz and Tradition* exemplifies the concerns and goals that will inform the series on Holocaust and Genocide Studies.

This series has its point of departure in the conviction that the Holocaust was a transformational event, one which has radically altered the condition of the historical world in which modern humans dwell. The systematic extermination of six million Jews, and the destruction of at least five million non-Jews (homosexuals, the mentally and physically handicapped, Gypsies, Slavs, etc.), all designated as *Untermenschen* (sub-humans) by the Nazis, in large part through ghastly efficient techniques of industrialized slaughter in factories of death, of which Auschwitz was emblematic, constitutes a *novum* of the twentieth century. It is this *novum*, and its far-reaching implications for our modernity, that the volumes in the series on Holocaust and Genocide Studies will attempt to grasp.

In addition to its character as a transformational event, one which has literally reshaped the human landscape, we believe that the Holocaust must be grasped in prospective, not just retrospective, terms. This special series on Holocaust and Genocide Studies, will grapple with the possibility that the Holocaust, beyond its many features which were historically unique to Nazism and the Hitler-state, was also an expression of tendencies deeply rooted in the historical trajectory of modernity. In that sense, we must be alert to the prospect that the Holocaust opened a door into a social world in which genocide may have become an ever present objective-real-possibility, one which can become constitutive of the socio-economic, political, and cultural matrix. The Holocaust, symbolized by the smokestacks of Auschwitz, opened a door into a death-world, and in the waning years of the twentieth century, nearly fifty years after the destruction of the Nazi regime, that door remains open. Humans today dwell in a social world in which new technicized death worlds, new genocides, may invade their future. It is this danger, and the need for thinking to comprehend it, that will be a constant preoccupation of the editors of this series on Holocaust and Genocide Studies.

Between Auschwitz and Tradition gives form to the concerns and preoccupations that will animate this special series. For Watson, Auschwitz is the great divide, the abyss, that separates modern humans from their ancestors. Today, we all inhabit what Watson designates as "Planet Auschwitz." However, in a world shorn of all transcendental warrants, we lack the intellectual and cultural bases to confront this brute *factum*. Watson believes that metaphysics, in both its traditional and modernist forms, both obscures the dimensions of the transformation wrought by the Holocaust, and is complicitous with it. As a result, for Watson, the "Nazi self" cannot be limited to the leaders of the Hitler-state, or to the Arendtian desk killers who planned the Final Solution, or even to Christopher Browning's "ordinary men" who were prepared to massacre innocent human beings, or to brutally shove them onto the cattle cars that would transport them to Auschwitz. In a daring move, Watson insists that the Nazi self may be within us, the end result of the atomization, and truncated public life, that is one hallmark of our now global techno-scientific civilization. This Nazi self, of course, is not all we are, but it is a monstrous aspect of ourselves. As a result, for Watson, the danger of human-made mass death is not over, it did not perish with the Third Reich, but continues in the "terror of an Auschwitz nations-world which murders and fabricates indifference to crime as easily as it did the earlier death camps."

Between Auschwitz and Tradition is an effort to confront that Nazi self, as it is made manifest in its various images, and texts; and an attempt to re-image, and re-construct ourselves. As an effort at both deconstruction, and re-imaging, Watson's work blends philosophical, literary, socio-political, and theological reflections on the Holocaust. In repudiating the rigid separation of the disciplines, Watson also challenges the traditional literalness, and linearity of the text itself. His use of his own photographs as an integral part of his work opens the act of reading to image, sign, and vision— all with the aim of finally liberating ourselves from the Nazi labyrinth.

In a work that will challenge many cherished assumptions by its insistence that we all inhabit Planet Auschwitz, and contain a Nazi self within our collective being, Watson has by no means fallen into despair. The Nazi self is not the final self, or the destined form of humankind. *Between Auschwitz and Tradition* is a transgression of the shapes, forms, and "laws," of Planet Auschwitz. As such, it will set the tone for this special series on Holocaust and Genocide Studies.

Alan Milchman and Alan Rosenberg

acknowledgements

I want to especially thank the following friends and colleagues for their encouragement, assistance, careful readings and critical suggestions: Eugene Gendlin, Véronique Fóti, Elliot Levine, Alan Milchman, Jesse Nash, James O'Meara, Alan Rosenberg, and Robert Scharff.

The moral and financial support of the Holocaust Educational Foundation and its President, Theodore Weiss, have been invaluable. My association with them is one of those wonderful connections that take us beyond the Auschwitz legacy.

And my wonderful students of "Auschwitz and After"—they do not know how important they are in the formation and articulation of their teachers' thoughts.

Mary Marocco, Theresa Mysing, and Elizabeth Nguyen are very patient and understanding "models."

Mr. and Mrs. Solomon Radasky have testified before my "Auschwitz and After" class for the last eight years and given so very generously of their time and special knowledge to my students. They have made my feeble pedagogic attempts at teaching the Holocaust into something closer to a dialogue with the most pressing issue of this century. This is my second-hand response to what both of you bear with so much courage and dignity.

The Way of Insight

Two Faces of Realism

INTRODUCTION

The Nazi death camps forever changed everything. Whether acknowledged or not, within the formation of Auschwitz we have become different from anything that has ever been written about us. In the last fifty years we have changed more than in the last five thousand. Suddenly, a discontinuity called Auschwitz separated us from the world of our ancestors. Our new world is Planet Auschwitz, an unworld with satellites as separate and incommunicable as the distant world of our ancestors. Everything coming through the cold space separating us from the tradition must now be heard with new ears, very suspicious ears sensitized to the boot beats of marching postmen. The hermeneutical circle of these two worlds has an abyss at its center. The danger lies in crossings that cross-over this abyss, ignoring it and thus serving its nihilating appropriation.

Yes, we have mutated. So suddenly in fact that the stuff of which we are formed bears the trauma of this shock as a wound that may fold over but never heal. We are a massive mutating trauma which ranges from the depths of its repression to the heights of those all too few bodies who remember, testify, and think against all odds of undoing this repression. The repression keeps us from thinking, binding us instead to cynicism and nostalgia. It is also that part of us which wants to kill off the other parts that bring the pain of remembrance, the pain of wounded thinking.

When the world became Planet Auschwitz, its inmates were left with only one connection to one another—the only one permitted by the selection process. Our life-world is that very tenuous connection of already condemned, survivors, and those yet to be selected. That connection is our only lifeline, our only means of escaping a progressively refined nihilistic process of destruction, and our only means of destroying it. Face-to-face with this destruction process, its administrators, and its survivors, we are very different from our ancestors in the old world. Facing the real possibility of extinction, we know we have only problematic resources for escaping. Our mutated self is so problematic, so contingent, it can never succumb to what are now old world fictions of a non-problematic self. We mutations must rewrite everything that has been projectively written about us in the old world. All traditional transcendental warrants were vaporized in the Nazi crematoria and the cultural instruments that today make-up their legacy. Not only is there no guarantee of salvation, it is no longer even probable.

What was done and what we have become is not over; it continues as the legacy of destruction. It will never be over. We will never be done with this legacy. We have become monstrously implicated in the terror of an Auschwitz nations-world which murders and fabricates indifference to crime as easily as it did the earlier death camps. The only question now is whether we can transform this terror and begin a post Auschwitz era, an era of remembrance without state-sponsored institutions of destruction. An era of remembrance because we will live forever with the possibility of state-sponsored and philosophically legitimated mass murder.

Toward this new era, nothing of what has been done can be denied, nothing can be left to work its murderous implications in the depths of repressions so easily induced by the powers of state. Relentlessly deconstructive, our survival and transformation beyond the monstrous depends upon our rejection of all finalities. This is the reserve of our troubled self, the reserve we are face-to-face with the disaster and its survivors. Facing the testimonies, we have no right to despair. That is our new inheritance, our reserve with which we can move beyond the cynical pale of realism and the evasive encapsulations of idealism. Everything that has been written must be brought to this new site of surviving, against the monstrous thing which wants to implicate us in its crimes before it annihilates us.

But surviving and opposing the on-going disaster is not how most people see themselves. Most learned professionals do not think of themselves this way. For them and most "normal" people, the Shoah, the Holocaust, Auschwitz, are things of the past, over and done with. The faces of the survivors are not their faces, not their everyday face-to-face. And this is why they confront a world of stubborn indifference. It is a new and monstrous world, a world in which terror confronts everyone who begins to face its realities. Terrorized, we do not want to acknowledge that we have mutated, have become problematic selves without certainties, without homelands, without the transcendental warrants or guarantees of Christianized culture, and thus always imperiled by the technical and philosophic powers of state.

Even worse, facing that terror we know that opposition to those powers cannot dispense with precisely the philosophy, literature, religion and science forming the legacy of destruction. But it is the tradition which must be taken back from its appropriation by the powers of destruction, and it cannot be taken back without passing through the transformation of our mutated being. It is of course easier to deny this *feuerbach* and bathe instead in the cooler nostalgia of the easy translations. Easier, that is, until the executioners call for another selection.

For the most part, the testimonies of the survivors have not broken through the terror-induced indifference of business as usual. We know the sad response all too well: "What happened was terrible, but it is past. The victors have insured that nothing remains of all that. There is today nothing left of those institutions, and thus nothing remains that would demand a complete rethinking and reordering of human affairs." The abyss has been crossed-over, and covered with a mark that terrorizes anyone attempting to think otherwise.

Indifference today is driven, moved by powerful forces of repression and terror. And it is these forces that carry forth the "normal" business of administered and state-sanctioned death. As repressed beings, we live by the grace of forces that mark for extinction everything other than what it designates as proper. The improper, the impure, the mutant is what these forces mark for annihilation, beyond any kind of recovery/memory. What the repression conceals is that these forces have marked everything and everyone for annihilation. The repressive forces of the Auschwitz legacy are the culminating forces of nihilism.

On the earth become Planet Auschwitz everything and everyone are made equivalent: the totality equals zero. In ways that are still not well understood, this universal equivalence is the foreclosure of the Western intellectual tradition, a tradition foreclosed so as to render it immune to our mutated interpretations. Foreclosure keeps the tradition away from the transformative event of the disaster. The old world tradition is foreclosed by refusals to interpret that tradition with the exigencies of our mutated context. Thus, in lieu of responding to what we have become, the foreclosed tradition throws us into a recursive loop that repeats over and over again its completion in the establishment of universal equivalence. This endless ending is the antithesis of responsibility, a loop that reiterates "the good" helplessly and cynically. It is "here," in the impossible non-coincidence of loop and witnessing, that the survivors attempt the impossible—to bear testimony in a world whose heart has been hardened by the universal equivalence of everything and everyone. By means of this wretchedness-making-equivalents machine, the narrations of the disaster are each and every one fashioned into the same commodity in an endless series of harmless fabulations. The kids can learn about the Holocaust, recite the litany of "Never Again!" and get on with the task of finding their proper place in the loop of business-as-usual.

This loop is, however, like all nooses—it can face only what it has fabricated. What is within the loop is not made by the equivalent maker. The loop faces only victims who finally acknowledge its inevitability. But then there is no need for the loop because the loop desires precisely those whose refusal denies the loop the recognition it needs. Rebellious survivors in the loop of business as usual are both the scandal of the loop and its hidden desire. As these witnesses come forward, slipping into the noose of fabulations, the equivalent maker goes to work making the indifference that isolates these intruders. Thus the survivors hang suspended in the abyss between Auschwitz and tradition Within this loop we are all survivors, but we need not remain disconnected from those whose testimonies disturb indifference.

The loop both succeeds and fails.

Somehow the witnesses keep coming, bearing testimony within the same machinery that annihilated their families. They are greeted by indifference. But there are moments when the wretched machinery of universal equivalence fails to conceal its legacy—the death camps, where children were burned alive to save the two-fifths of cent more it would have cost to gas them. The loop stays tied, but momentarily we see the noose that snared those who went up in the smoke of the crematoria. Then, recovery: business as usual and forgetfulness.

But recovery is also momentary. After those brief glimpses, the essence of manifestation has become troubled. Uneasiness is joined with indifference. The moments of recognition linger, returning unexpectedly. We see and listen to survivors: "You went through hell." Then, recovery: "We must do lunch some time." But, then, unexpectedly, that chilling Nazi phrase about remaining decent through it all comes out of the abyss. The loop fails in these moments of recognition, when vulnerability touches the non-indifference between "them" and us. In a strange and powerful way, a connection is momentarily recognized despite the rule of machinery that specializes in disconnections.

Today, which is the same as yesterday in the rule of equivalence, we troubled ones must face both the administrators of this business of extinction and the many who prefer a contented and settled life at degree zero to a troubled one of remembrance. The voting public doesn't like the monsters of remembrance. Better the machines be fed their requirements. This is more than the necessity of sacrifice; it is the cynicism of a public that kills everything that unsettles the easiness of its repressed existence. The production machine of business and life as usual is an anti-remembrance mechanism that substitutes indifference for responsibility. And this is how it disconnects us from ourselves and one another. What is at stake is not some immutable life-world, but a severely impaired one—the only shared basis we have left to escape universal extinction.

To remember, then, is to return to the terrible annihilating machine and stand within its generated indifference, testifying against every one of its foreclosures, and protesting every one of its displacements. Remembrance is standing-in not just for the extinguished, but for our own soul in this hardened world of abstract equivalents. Our un-world has become so wretched with injustice, so helpless with its "good," that it serializes its atrocities and demonstrates its "concern" by insisting that none deserve preferential "treatment." There is no abyss, only "problems."

Normal, everyday life is governed by this equal opportunity atrocity machine. The "concern" that it elicits after its crimes is even more obscene than the crimes themselves. The Holocaust, according to the loop, was just another of many atrocities. By modern comparative and statistical standards, six million does not top the list of atrocity casualties. But fairness does dictate its proper serialization in the state-approved history texts.

Serialization of atrocity is truly an advance on the failed Nazi attempt to eradicate the memory of the disaster. Today, forgetting follows in the wake of tons of documents, numerous films, plays, novels, even published testimonies, because each and every one is made equivalent to the many other atrocities and their records. The more one reads the serializations, the harder it is to discern the significance of any one: the total equals zero. What is left are the memories of the old world "translated" as equivalents of our forgetfulness. What is forgotten with all this equivalent information is the abyss at the center of the hermeneutical circle. The translation is an easy one because it crosses-over and by-passes the abyss. Thus we are handed this easy "translation" and expected to do the traditional thing: subsume the disaster as another of those terrible but necessary events in the history of Being. The old metaphysics is intact and working. This is the modernism that must be exposed, opposed, and re-written.

Standing-in is rebellion against this foreclosure and easy translation of tradition. Against all odds, the point of standing-in is to signify otherwise while in the scene of the foreclosure. It is the imaging of a testimony that shows the deadliness of the foreclosed tradition and its business as usual. We must signify otherwise, against the institutionalization of death, against a life whose "between" has been collapsed into an identity of being and nothing. This is the identity, the agony of the undead who procreate hopelessly, only to enforce the Auschwitz code of equivalence: innocence and unpredictable becoming is forbidden. There is, according to the loop, nothing unusual between birth and death. The foreclosing of the tradition institutes the rule of death.

Yes, death rules, but it is a death-rule masked by many idols. The system of death animated by idolatry, cynical thought, and the equivalent-making that reduces everything to ashes on the foreheads of fair-minded mourners is not trouble free. There are monsters in the belly of this beast, protesting its foreclosure of a future beyond wretchedness. What troubles the rule of death is the mutants, the problematic ones, insisting on uneasy translations of the old (and new) texts.

Between every text, every sentence, attached to every independent clause, there is a disaster. A troubled present—uneasy reading without traditional canons to insure authoritative renditions. Childhood's end comes today from that time when children whose parents and grandparents adhered to a troubling belief were burned alive. It was thus decided that the innocence of becoming will not be allowed on Planet Auschwitz. No play, equivalence, no nonsense: _ _ _ _ _ _ _ will be eradicated, forgotten for all time, according to a code insisting that the innocence of becoming must be sacrificed for the sake of the requirements of a thinking that cannot be upset, undone, or surprised by anything. Childhood's end was the foreclosure of our future. That future—a new beginning—lies in the figure of children we no longer resent for what we could have been.

Idolatry replaced the innocence of becoming, children and play, and an unforeseeable future. Everywhere, images that do not image replace uneasy ones. These easy images tell us things, definite things, easy things. Idolatry abolishes ambiguity, the troubling uncertainty of a remembrance that refuses all idolatry. Imaging is upsetting for those who crave images they can appropriate. The idol is a captivating captive of the repressed. Until, that is, something happens to make these easy images uneasy.

The persecutors of this wayward, uncertain, but committed imaging are apposite; the idolators are sure of themselves—nothing surprises them. No atrocity takes them back from the psychic security of their graven images—bodies of knowledge built-up on monstrous murder sites. Nothing stops this infernal damnation of innocence . . . nothing except the fools who stand-in without guarantees of salvation. On what authority? Only that of images imaging . . . uneasy imaging of images within normalized images of death.

That uneasiness happened to me—a happening that I could not shrug off. I tried, but soon everything, including writing, became as uneasy as the imagings that unveiled the idols of easy existence on Planet Auschwitz.

Not so gradually, certain thinkers became much uneasier—thinkers who were not shocked by the disaster and its repressions. In particular, and especially, there was Heidegger, from whom I had learned so much. I was taken aback by his certainty, his adeptness in crossing-over the disaster. When I first heard of his 1949 lecture in which he said that the essence of the death camps was the same as that of mechanized food production, I was dismayed that this great thinker of Time-Being could so easily subsume the disaster's radical impairment of our life-world under a categorical formulation referring to the problematic of industrialization. For Heidegger, nothing had happened in the death camps requiring a rethinking of problems posed by his earlier lectures and publications. For Heidegger, the configuration of the *Seinsfrage* remained unchanged by Auschwitz, the essence of which was prefigured by the industrialization of agriculture: nothing had happened requiring any modification of the structure of Dasein set forth in *Sein und Zeit.*

Heidegger was right about the thread of continuity running from industrialization to the death camps, but his essentializing of that continuity both crossed-over the abyss opened forever by Auschwitz and the impairment of our life-world by that opening. *Sein und Zeit* could no longer be read the way it might have been before Auschwitz. If Heidegger was unwilling or unable to do so, we must bring Heidegger's project for the destruction of the history of western ontology to the abyss and rewrite the existential analytic of Dasein.

Uneasily I came to see that Heidegger's Being and its self-withdrawing disclosure was not the same in the disaster-world as in the world he envisioned, untroubled by the images coming from the East. Could Heidegger's "history of Being" face the challenges of the disaster-world? How could a troubled self read Heidegger without those images? To continue with Heidegger, his "Dasein" would have to undergo a mutation.

Heidegger remained unflappable, but his writings are another matter. Heidegger, remember, came from both Planet Auschwitz and the old world. It was his mutated self that he could not accept, could not turn suspiciously toward his old self by connecting with the survivors. What he saw instead was the idolatry that would soothe his and our wounded flesh. After the disastrous event, he tried, accordingly, to bring a message from the old world across the cold and empty spaces separating the worlds. He knew the abyss was there between the two worlds, but he displaced it, projecting it backwards to the beginnings of technical thought in Plato and Aristotle. In other words, he used the abyss for a project he had begun in the 1920s. Or, we could say, Heidegger translated/transported the abyss from the between into/to his metaphysical vocabulary of the old world. This is the scandal behind his one published statement about the Holocaust in 1949. It is also, perhaps, the price for "authenticity."

There are, however, many deceptive messages being delivered to us. Many of them offer variations on Heidegger's displacement of the abyss, or some other way of avoiding that which must be gone through. Most, however, are not as "good" as Heidegger's. Heidegger displaced the disaster, but his writings struggle with that displacement. In his writings Heidegger's displacement of the abyss can be read by us mutants as uneasy with itself.

Our mutated body is sensitive to displacements of the abyss. Traumatized flesh is never indifferent to where and how it is being transported. Displacements take place as relocations under the cover of night. The propriety of the displacement conceals, makes ob-scene the relocation. Displacement, in other words, is an authorization of deportations that comes not only from Heidegger's pen. Deportation is an image within Heidegger's images of Being, as negativity and Dasein's resolute response (thinking Being). It is a troubling image not solely of Heidegger's making. If Dasein is the shepherd of Being, it cannot respond to Being's "sendings" as arranged by one untroubled conductor.

It is precisely our implication in Heidegger's texts that troubles them, pulling them back from their displacement. Traumatized flesh cannot read itself indifferently. We are different from anything that has been written about us but we are not apart from any of it. There is no purity, no standing-in that is apart from the evil of Planet Auschwitz and its delivery of deceptive messages from the old world. Which is not to say that some don't want that purity, that redemption, that release from wretchedness.

Many of us wanted it, but rejected it nonetheless. Perhaps, because we heard about the postcards sent by the Nazis to the relatives and loved ones of those about to perish in the death camps. Perhaps, something like that connected with other more current "postcards." There is plenty of "evidence" and none of it is admissible in the courts of Planet Auschwitz: *Le Différend*.

So there will be the purists, the redeemed ones, who judge Heidegger in serializations produced by the universal equivalence machine. Fools like ourselves must image *with and against* his images of Time-Being. Images within images, reversing, changing, undoing one another, giving birth to new ones—the innocence of imaging/becoming always mindful, always remembrance of what cannot be possessed. No bridge will ever successfully span the abyss. The *feuerbach* must be gone through, not over.

The disaster overtook Heidegger and his "work." There is evidence of this in Heidegger's writings, but there is also evidence that this overtaking was itself overtaken by the idolatry of Being, albeit a Being severely wounded by its "self"-encounter. Nevertheless, there is an unflappability in Heidegger that concerns Dasein and its historical mission. This unflappability lies at the heart of Heidegger's adherence to idolatry, and thus to his opposition to the innocence of becoming (Nietzsche). Heidegger foreclosed on Nietzsche, and not just Nietzsche. Which is why we who stand-in cannot foreclose on Heidegger and his foreclosures.

Given the acts of cowardice, irresponsibility, and what can only be called a calculated political attempt at displacement and transference of guilty complicity in the events of the "affaire Heidegger"—and not just in France—I want to be as clear as possible concerning my face-to-face with Heidegger. If Heidegger was guilty, and I believe he was, then so are all of us who read him as if nothing *essential* had happened. And if Heidegger was guilty, he was guilty because he thought within the drama which is Europe and the western intellectual tradition. The wholesale complicity of the western democracies in the Nazi process of destruction is ample evidence that we all dwell in that drama.

Yes, Heidegger came up short; he refused to stand nakedly exposed to the abyss. Heidegger's guilt lies in the fact that he failed to accept the Shoah as a transformative event. Instead, Heidegger displaced its urgency by subsuming it as an instance of the forgetfulness of Being—that was the requirement of his thinking. For that displacement we must hold **Heidegger and his writings** responsible. But settling the "affaire Heidegger" would be a foreclosure as deadly as the ones executed by Heidegger, and not just by Heidegger.

There are those who point accusatory fingers at Heidegger and wiggle them at those of us who still read him, as if their fingers weren't rewriting the worse parts of Heidegger's foreclosing texts with their double-crossing motions. By comparison (re-reading and re-writing), Heidegger's failings seem more like giant steps toward a possible acknowledgment of the transformative event. Behind these accusations, and not very far behind them, is the complicitous drive towards business as usual, towards serialized equivalents. Heidegger's involvement with the Nazis is unforgivable; it was a grave failing. But he was not alone. There were other thinkers that failed, and there are many today that continue to fail by displacing their responsibility onto Heidegger's failures and displacements.

Even more unforgivable is Heidegger's subsequent failure to acknowledge his failing. The most unforgivable in and of Heidegger's thought proceeds from its (Hegelian) totalization of the Western philosophical tradition. It was Heidegger's profound lack of humility, openness, and his unwillingness to acknowledge the vulnerability of his own thought that prompted his essentializing reduction of the Holocaust. But that is exactly why the postmodern task of thinking is to image Heidegger's images of the tradition through the abyss separating us from it. Heidegger's "fix" (foreclosure) of the tradition must be unfixed.

I say "must" to those who are aware they have been transformed by the event—to its old and new witnesses—and against the "effect" that is now working in everything political, social, intellectual, as well as in our private lives. Perhaps this alteration can only be acknowledged by those of us (the "semiterates") who now understand that we are without transcendental warrants, without the blessings of any "election." For the semiterates, the Auschwitz legacy is the idolatry that surrounds us and threatens to turn us all, spirit first, into ashes.

But this means that Heidegger (and not just Heidegger) must be read, reread, deconstructed, re-written. And then we must repeat all that again, always again, suspiciously undoing what we have done in response to irresponsibility and indifference. After Auschwitz, we must recognize that responsibility is endless, a debt that cannot be repaid in full.

This is not understood by those now suggesting that we should not or need not read Heidegger. Nor is it understood by those who read Heidegger and simply repeat him. Now, especially now, is the time to refuse any and all sacralizations of Heidegger, as well as all projections of guilt, terror, and complicity onto a thinker fallen victim to the mass media, its hacks, and the states it serves so very well. For the mass media, the linking of deconstruction to the holding responsible of Heidegger and his writings is tantamount to compounding the neo-fascist conspiracy it already sees so clearly in the case of Heidegger and his readers. And not just for the mass media, as we have recently seen in the brutal and intellectually shoddy attacks on Derrida for his support of his friend, the one-time collaborator Paul De Man. What seems clear to me, however, is that Levinas (and his readings/imagings of Heidegger, et al.) and Derrida (and his imagings/readings of Heidegger, de

Man, et al.) are showing us the way of responsible and necessary intellectual activity after Auschwitz. But such responsibility understands its complicity. There is no responsible writing after-Auschwitz-about-Auschwitz unmarked by its formations.

Much must be done if we are to survive, and what must be done will be profoundly different than what has been handed down to us by way of tradition. The impairment of our life-world and the absence of guaranteed salvation are not negative characteristics. Our retrieve of the tradition through the abyss will re-make that tradition in our own uneasy image, which means that it will become, among many other changes, irreversibly multivocal and thus incompletable. This is what Heidegger's retrieve missed and had to miss after he crossed-over the abyss.

By 1942 the image of Dasein's authentic being-towards-its-own-end could no longer be the same one that came to us from those facing their end in the Nazi death camps. Mortality is one thing and state sponsored and executed mass murder of an isolated people is another. But it is these two images that must image together in any re-reading/writing of Heidegger. They are different images but they are also connected images—terrifyingly connected.

After the decisions made by the Nazi state in the spring of 1941, the phenomenon of death could no longer be understood as being-towards-the-end in the sense of an authentic non-relational possibility because this "end" had been taken-over, appropriated by state power. For those trapped within the Nazi orbit of destruction, Heidegger's "resoluteness" could only mean acceptance of their isolation by the world's indifference to their fate. The indifference of the world had become their non-relational "possibility." To be resolute, in the sense of Heidegger's 1927 formulations, would make their death without meaning, without traces, without protest. It would mean their willingness to "authentically" embrace the indifference that denied everything signified by their collective existence. Their "resolute" death, in other words, would be a complicitous acceptance of the powers and "truth" of the murderous state. Resoluteness would thereby transform individual suicide into a people's collective embrace of their own non-meaning, their own cancellation without traces. Such resoluteness would be the ultimate Nazi victory, one which the New Church had been unable to achieve without Nazi state power.

The power of the Nazi state and the world-wide indifference regarding its "Jews" had either shipwrecked the fundamental ontology project of *Sein und Zeit*, or revealed its "ontological-ontic" ramifications for peoples cast outside the protection of the dominant nation states. Imaging with these composite images is the concretion of authenticity. And when concretized in the figure of isolated Jews, authenticity becomes obscene. Even more obscene is the image of Jews facing-their-non-relational-end as a self-

willing that reiterates their expulsion from the Nazi state and the indifference of other states to that expulsion and its implications. The second image
is the image sought by the state: self-effacement of the Jews—the Jews as
sacrificial victims of their "own" history.

With these composite images we come upon the failings of Heidegger's
politics: he formulates an authentic, social Dasein that is otherwise than and
perhaps opposed to political being-together. Dasein's "community" is
without the necessary contingencies of togetherness which make up any
postmodern political community. For Heidegger, such contingencies and
the protections they offer are part of the inauthentic "they-self." Dasein'
community is, quite to the contrary, always its "own," radically privatized,
always non-relational. Which is why Dasein, the caller of the "call of
conscience," says "*nothing* which might be talked about, gives no information about events." To be authentic is to be made ready for extermination.
This is the authenticity that the murderous state fully endorses and recom-
mends to both its victims and survivors.

The Call of Authenticity

This can be said another way: Heidegger's formulation of authenticity in his
early texts can only apply to a people whose existence is not threatened by
the powers of the modern nation state; that is, authenticity is a characteristic
only of "historical" peoples whose temporality has a transcendental warrant
(an ontological link with Being) and thus makes of them a mythic people.
The images within images we have mentioned (deportation, expulsion,
extermination) make the very concept of *Da-Sein* problematic. Within his

texts, "we" problematic ones meet only a mythic people signifying beyond the pale of contingencies and the chance events and associations that make up our inauthentic political community. Which is why Heidegger, always the opponent of idle chatter, will stand firm in his resolute commitment to the greatness of the national socialist movement. It is the plurality of the human community that his fundamental ontology cannot embrace. If the *Seinsfrage* lies only at the center of Europe, then its essence is as ashen as the manufactured corpses of Auschwitz.

Even after the war, Heidegger steadfastly denies the face of Others, those without guaranteed salvation, without a historical mission and onto-logical link with Being. He refuses a thinkers' dialogue with Paul Celan, who later dies facing everything living turned to stone. And that image is also one we must bring together with Heidegger's images. Otherwise, like Heideg-ger, we would steadfastly refuse to meet the unimaginable, the abysmal separation of worlds, with anything but handy subsumptions of every "equivalent" atrocity. Do we really want to subsume Heidegger, the man found guilty in word and deed, under a category of failing that somehow does not apply to ourselves when we do that? Do we, in other words, want to believe that we belong to a people with transcendental warrants? Do we want to continue to believe that we are the "new elect," one nation under God? Do we want to condemn Heidegger but continue his texts as the unread that leads us to our reward? If so, that nostalgia will lead us to the gas chambers, either as victim or administrator.

These are not rhetorical questions since it is precisely the texts that are being waylaid by the sensations of the "affaire Heidegger." These are the texts that must be read in the context of their times and ours and reread again and again with the images coming from the abyss between these contexts. It is the coincidental incommensurability of these texts, the images within the images, that cannot be read in-differently. The time of a context is never *its* time, but, as Levinas has shown, the time of the other.

When the documents of the Holocaust are placed next to Heidegger's texts of the 1940s, the author Heidegger becomes other than the man who stood apart from the destruction process while thinking the inception of philosophy in a retrieve of Heraclitus, Parmenides, and Hölderlin. The northeasterly wind that carries the ashes of the burning children toward Freiburg and the inception of philosophy brings the philosopher into a whirlwind utterly different than the parabolic orbit of the retrieved incep-tion. The juxtaposition of these incommensurable texts has yet to be published.

This juxtaposition is a matter of imaging beyond the idols that support the rule of death. We have mutated and our troubled flesh will not permit us to be "categorially prepared" for atrocity. If the Holocaust is the essence of the west, this essence holds only in easy readings of the old world. The end of innocence and becoming may well be the end of philosophy, but mutated thinking begins when we respond to this completion as something marked by the abyss which easy readings of the old world philosophy have not gone through. Easy metaphysics may have led to Auschwitz, and may indeed be capable of dwelling in it, but it cannot lead away from it. **The completion of easy philosophy lies in its incapacity to meet the center of the two worlds**. According to easy philosophy, the essence of the west is revealed as its incapacity to face the unimaginable with anything but idols and masked truths. We mutants, however, are too suspicious for such easy "truths."

The following texts/images were prepared over a period of twelve years, some of them pre-dating the recent revival of the "affaire Heidegger." Although, all have been many times revised, sometimes expanded and sometimes considerably shortened, I have made no attempt to "attune" them with the tones and overtones of the current Heidegger et. al. affair. Taken together these texts are the testimony of one wounded mutation attempting to face a very problematic self. So problematic in fact that the texts/images are not, could not be purely autobiographical. There are many connections, links, with the "fictional"—with the traditionally excluded. There are images within images, with shifting positions, each examining the others and sometimes resisting each other. Above all, they attempt to image beyond the fixities (idols) which hold us back from seeing the task that faces us in this monstrous world of administered death. Thus they speak, directly and indirectly, a politics other than the old world politics of natural kinds, kin folks, tribes, and the even more vicious oedipal societies of our brave new liberal nation states and the new world order.

Since there more than a few people who still adhere to the doctrine of natural kinds and kin folks, it is imperative to show human solidarity as other than identity, propriety, and authenticity. I learned this by becoming a "jew," a survivor and enemy of the monstrous equivalence maker. That I became a "jew" will raise some hackles among some of the believers in natural kinds. I did not convert since I had nothing to convert from. I have always been without kind, but I did not always know this. It was not so kindly pointed out to me. Was I then nostalgic? Yes, but I got over that as I learned how to speak and listen to others whose own voice was excluded by the tradition-made-easy and its privileged signifying subject.

I became jew in the terror of the on-going Holocaust and its survivors. And as such, I could only respond without the explanations, theories, justifications, and excuses that are the prerogatives of membership in organizations untroubled by the persistence of mass murder. Instead, and unashamedly, I respond by not so simply substituting the solidarity of resisters who speak in many voices for the propriety of unified theories. Becoming jew, as I understand it, is to affirm self as a plurality without a sum, a context resisting all unifications. Such plurality has many effects, not the least of which is mutated and mutilated writing, which in turn problematizes the very representations which would otherwise denote one's (proper) place under the sun. We are all without "kind" but never alone in that. Human solidarity is a contingency without transcendental guarantees—it is the fragility and vulnerability that prompts writing differently in the facelessness of indifference.

Mutated writing lacks old world authority and its transcendental warrants. Admittedly, with concessions to current levels of repression, to write without such warrants is to invite Voltaire's charge of being an "Epicurean pessimist." Oxymoronic or not, the following texts do not enlist unbound transcendental warrants. The title of Facet 1 is to be taken in its twofold and oppositional sense: semiterate, a person who writes in a context where oppositions and even contradictions can never be unified in a grand theory or practice. Camus called such situations absurd. My version of Camus' "absurd" is the abyss between the old and new worlds. It is precisely the lack of bridges that testifies to the sheer givens of non-natural, contingent, and pluralistic groupings. This is, I believe, what Camus meant by human solidarity. Without it, as he warned, we will continue to kill one another for the best of old (easy) world reasons.

As a mutant jew I cannot stand safely above the destruction process and write "about" it. Thus the following texts are not loaded with competentia and essentia. We have seen the results of these legitimatization techniques. Our solidarity, our impaired life-world makes us suspicious of everything sublime. As an artist, I was deeply influenced by the modernist insistence that the pictorial surface remain pure, that all representational and historical references must be excluded so that its "immediacy" shines only for the sake of art and beauty. But the specialist perspective of modern art and theory is a privileged position that can be embraced only at the expense of forsaking the voices of the many non-privileged others. To make beautifully pure surfaces in the age of atrocity is to render the excluded obscene. The specialist perspective is never neutral. Since the formation of the death camps, art which remains faithful to the modernist aesthetic is as complicitous with the forces of state-sponsored death as the bureaucrats who kept the trains on schedule. Both are merely conforming to their job descriptions.

Whoever gives the gift has no need of the gift. And it is always the human multivocal context which gives more than it needs; *although impaired, its plurality exceeds the scarcity of identity*. Even the "it" is plural. It is a mutant resistance to all laws, equations, totalities—a resistance that exceeds them. Mutant identity is thus like a place-marker that is always left behind to begin again the never ending story of remembrance. The move beyond modernism and specialization is anything but a loss.

Contingent human solidarity also replaces the identity of engendered patriarchy and its privileges. In some of the texts/images to follow this will raise the hackles of the firm and well-defined male gender—a very heavily repressed if less than sublime body.

The following texts/images are developmental in that they come to see economics, production, and business as usual as parts of the monstrous destruction process. To define "Jew" (and not only "Jew"), to decontextualize the contingencies of existence, to transfix the movements of multi- and polyvocal resistances, to equalize by transforming all varieties of exchange into economic exchange for the sake of accumulating and concentrating wealth—always for the sake of an idea, a truth, propriety, and transcendental warrants—is to erode our solidarity and impaired life-world. Camus and many others pulled up short of the Party as they came to understand that rebellion turns against itself when its embodied context is lost. The Party— the Communists, the Capitalists, the Bureaucrats, the Educators, the Professionals. Everywhere the Party. There is no escaping the destruction process, but our fragile, contingent solidarity is capable of steadfast resistance to its many overt and covert administrations.

Today everything that fails to give voice to the victims is part of the on-going destruction process. Without the resistance of a newly and necessarily formed solidarity, we will find ourselves too late facing the executioner, and there will be no transcendental high court to judge and condemn their final word. The reign of administered death rests upon propriety, which attempts to break everything that moves non-territorially. The monstrous today is the growing terror against the non-territorial and its unnatural groupings. To respond to terrorist selections is to take the other, **any other,** out of place and back into the non-natural community that resists the order of old (easy) world warrants. Such is the contingent and fragile responding resistance to modern idolatry and its murderous machinery.

A few words about style, which is never independent of the context of writing. If the world were whole and we did not live amidst the terrible effects of the splitting that has characterized the entire history of domination and mastery, it might be possible to make an art that could conceal its own artifice without endangering those its self-concealing withdrawal attracts to its luring traces. That was the presupposition of modernist art. Today, however, writing within the awareness of the on-going destruction process requires a postmodern art of writing, one which discloses its own means of representation. For the seamless web of seduction and theoretical closure we must substitute what many will first perceive as clumsier artifices. The visibility of syntax has become a personal-political necessity for our survival.

Art that confronts the separations and privileged groupings of a profoundly racist, patriarchal, and genocidal society cannot be comforting. Not can it be seamless without distorting the splits it confronts and reveals. Berel Lang has shown us how the Nazis contrived a language of domination by subjecting language itself to domination. By forcibly joining words and phrases that usually had little or no association with one another, this Nazi artifice of enforced conjunctions left audiences with the extreme alternatives of total acceptance or denial. Thus the German expression *Gleichschaltung* was transformed into a Nazi code word, shifting its meaning from the more or less neutral "unification" to "the process of bringing into line."

Above all, then, writing after Auschwitz requires gaps in the discourse, gaps which honest and caring discourse refuses to cross-over. Gaps (burning children, the unthought, and others such as the homeless and poor) will only be represented when the received ways of representation are rendered problematic by disturbing references and uneasy images that discredit the order producing these gaps. What is at stake is not the kinkiness of post-modernism, but whether or not we can see what we don't want to see otherwise than through the usual ways that make "crimes of logic" an inseparable and necessary part of the "real" world. The rescue of those hanging from the sides of the ruptures in our world has this transformation as a prerequisite.

Seeing who and what has been rendered invisible and unheard by privileged frames of reference and signification is not, however, a one-way communication. Gaps in the texts which follow are just as importantly my recognition that I can not speak for those more and differently imperiled than myself. In this sense, the gaps are invitations for others to speak, modify, transform and continue the discourse without being forced to either totally accept or reject this face-to-face encounter.

The sometimes awkward and always uneasy texts/images that follow take aim at the mythical powers of tradition in an attempt to get free of those powers of appropriation. I believe we can move beyond a hermeneutics of suspicion, but I also believe we must remain suspicious about that as well. Since representation has moved well beyond the naiveté of mirroring nature, we can no longer pretend to extricate ourselves from the effects of simulation and seduction. What we do have in the place of Nature, Truth, Reality, and the like is one another and the substitution of one for the other in the sometimes terrible situations of oppression and the sometimes wonderful celebrations of our communities of difference. In response to coherent totalities, resistance is a matter of mixing representations for the sake of differences and the richness of existence. The logic of death and destruction is overcome when that richness overwhelms the scarcity of meaning within the privileged frames of reference.

A major premise of "Between Auschwitz and Tradition" (BAT) is that centuries of intermingling and mutating discourses have formed elements of our selves, which achieved deadly self-form with the invention of the Nazi death camps and their state-bureaucratic administration of mass death. It is this Nazi self that resonates with the Event called the Shoah (Auschwitz, the Holocaust). On the one hand, there is our intense fascination with the Nazi type while, on the other hand, this fascination is thoroughly mingled with an equally intense horror at what this type made possible and accomplished.

Yeah!

The history and culture which we embody is what we experience with both fascination and horror as we face the Event. Self-recognition is what the Shoah provides.

BAT does not suggest that the composition of these elements in the figure of the Nazi is their only possible or destined form. But it does argue that this specific self must be undone if the achieved logic of domination and state-sponsored mass death is to be left without accomplices. The accomplished Nazi self is not the totality of what we are, but it is the most deadly aspect of ourselves. It is a figure that demands totalization of what we are, might have been, and can become. It is, in other words, a figure that transverses the traditional boundaries between self and other, truth and fabulation, private and public, good and evil. BAT attempts to come to terms with this monstrous "inner beast" by both facing its various images/texts and then reimaging these. Deconstructing fascist mytho-poetic fabulations is not enough. The Nazi self is not the final self. Transgressive alliances in solidarity against what remains of that self are matters of writing-imaging (ourselves) otherwise. This has much to do with the rather unusual style and format of the texts collected under the title BAT. They both deconstruct and reimage "self."

BAT is a series of texts blending philosophical, literary, socio-political, and theological reflections on the Shoah in a personal narrative that attempts to overcome the usual separation of these modes of inquiry. The elements/texts which are composed in the figure of the Nazi self cannot remain separated if "we" are to undo precisely the connections which made this configuration possible. Nor can they be left separated according to the traditional genres of fiction, poetry, philosophy, theology, science, and myth. The possible interweavings may be virtually limitless, but certain tracings must be followed and undone to liberate ourselves from the Nazi labyrinth.

Considerable demands are thus placed on the reader of these texts. It is not so much the violation of traditional academic boundaries but precisely the connections made that may invoke resistance to what is said. Even though the texts that compose BAT are personal, their meanderings are certain to occasion various kinds of self-recognition. And that, I hope, is one major point made by these texts: the boundary between the private person and effective political life is transgressed every time "we" undo the Nazi self. Undoing, in this sense, is constructive and empowering. With respect to the Nazi self, every illicit connection fractures the Auschwitz legacy.

The style(s) of these texts is thus self-consciously contra the formal "universality" of much academic writing. Contra because after Auschwitz, all impersonal forms of expression are masks of an unacknowledged self-implication in the service of the very forces attempting to promote business-as-usual. We must stop being examples of the Nazi type. Each of us, however, must do that by making other-connections.

Style and structure are intimately related, in ways that begin with the "personal" while struggling against the barrier to others. However, the desire to connect with others is fraught with dangers. Much of Part I (facets series) is concerned with these dangers, especially the philosophic danger of appropriating others under the egological framework of the same. The texts making up Facet 1 thus speak of new ways of writing/reading/speaking, all of which are collected under the designation "semiterate"—playing on the multiple senses and associations of the word (antisemitic, semi-literate). It is the "Hell of Subjectivity," the prison house of the (philosophic-authentic) self, that seems to hold us in bondage to monologue (fear of vulnerability and thus our failure to connect). "The Fine Style" takes aim at this monologue in its revolutionary guise (a personal confession, which I hope many will connect with). "Surfaces," introduced by a photographic image, begins the mutual supplementariness of image-text by connecting the traditional image of depth with the deadly abyss and suggesting instead the complexity of folding surfaces. The image is anti-patriarchal and introduces a certain "feminist" critique. The Nazi self is a patriarchal self.

Facet 2 retreats from semiterate playfulness and folding surfaces by recalling totalizing beliefs and the resentment they engender. The mood is nasty here, but anger and arrogance move towards "gravity and the real" and then into the abyss of the Event, which recalls what has been lost by this "lapse" into totalization, anger, arrogance, resentment—monotheistic compulsion. "Premature Transformation" is the first formulation of the task of thinking after the Event, but it does that by reminding us that the monotheistic compulsion is still in force.

Facet 3 reiterates the monotheistic compulsion, but now from its more secularized sides. It moves closer and closer to the fatal coincidence of this compulsion and its Nazi appropriation. This is the subject of "Being a Nazi," a combination of personal experience and fabulation which suggests, however, that "personal" experience is collective/shared rather than merely private/solitary. The postmodern character of the task of thinking after Auschwitz is introduced here. Thus "Dachau" is largely imaginal in character, attempting to image the terrible connections of town and concentration camp. We are reminded that new connections cannot by-pass or forget the old ones.

Facet 4 plays with the dangers of fabulation—new ways of thinking that are no longer "true" or "false." The tone is that of the new ways, in form of hints only, but still bothered by old desires for unity, totality, coherence, etc. Thus "trauming." "My calling" speaks of voices not yet quite "real," yet commanding. The Nazi self is going under and the multi-self emerging— "Intromission." This multi-self must now confront the un-transformed world.

Part II (waves series) "The Weakening" begins by remembering the Subject at the same time that the multi-self thinks against it. But thinking against is not postmodern thinking—"Adorno's memorandum." Poetry (of sorts) then serves as a prelude to a new way of seeing—"phoslegs." To remember, to bear witness, is impossible with the old ways of seeing and representation. To remember within the logic of domination would be to succumb to sacrilege and idolatry.

Wave 2 attempts to think other than as the Subject. What is suggested is that thinking this other way grants access to memories we would otherwise not have ("Mind yourself"). "Carnal hermeneutics" introduces a postmodern discourse on the body, a body that is fragmented and wounded, a body that makes no sense without that of others.

Part III (winds series) begins by replacing the old sense of coherence with body connectiveness—touching, crossing-over, healing—while noting resistances to this transformation. The Nazi self has mutated; it has new characteristics. But Nazi aspects are still there. "You never get enough if you're good" is a fabulated memory of a certain prerequisite training for becoming a Nazi. From the standpoint(s) of the multi-self it shows, however, that such training cannot completely determine self: the self becomes and is nothing more or less than that becoming. Becoming is innocent, but being something/one is not. This is the preface to "working," which indicates how matter contributes to what we form in the process of working. The material traces of the Shoah are thus "at work" in the world and in the imagery/texts which follow. This section is a critique of industrialism, mass production, and its eternal recurrence of the same (death) and connects industrialism with the monotheistic compulsion.

"J'accuse" continues to explicate the logic of domination operative in mass production and reproduction, attempting to show that remembrance works otherwise. "A Nietzschean tale" images Freud together with Nietzsche contra the readings of Freud which separate him from this "other." Here, and in the section "why the rational is not real," thinking moves away from "bodies of knowledge" (the packaged tradition) over to the place of others. This movement of crossing-over is then repeated in the personal memory narrated in "a grammatical note."

"Drawing on Barthes the semiographist" develops a new way of thinking about writing/drawing and working with rather than against materiality. Several images are drawn-together: writing/drawing/the domination of women/my Luger/desire and the pen(is)/Kiefer's materialized surfaces/Erté's alphabet.

"Wayward winds" emphasizes the experimental character of this new way of writing/drawing and argues how the traditional way of thinking pulls us away from this vulnerability. Academic philosophy is the target here—a personal note. "Normalcy" continues this critique while attempting to bring the personal (faces) into the foreground of our thinking.

"Repetition compulsion" and "America the beautiful" are concerned with the normalization of mass death in everyday life and its industrialized forgetfulness—a forgetfulness with cynical consequences (story on p. 168).

"Mirror imaging" speaks again of/in a way different from that of the Subject, his authenticity, and his bodies of knowledge and belief. Heidegger's failure is recalled as a paradigmatic image of the Subject. "Dead-ins?" simply states the new "position" I have come to occupy, together with its new ways of thinking-imaging. It is an uneasy image that calls for the reader's implication in its complex movement.

notes

The Auschwitz legacy is not anathema to writing philosophical essays, books and scholarly articles for learned journals. Quite the contrary. To the extent that thinkers do not confront this legacy and write responsively, the legacy continues under the cover of business as usual. Unfortunately, there are more than a few who believe that the Shoah requires neither a transformation of how we think nor any change in how we represent the world.

Thus works like Camus' *L'homme révolté* remain exceptional, especially when one remembers that this particular work was published in 1951. Jean-Paul Sartre chastised Camus for drawing the connecting lines between political agendas and terrorism and for his failure to privilege leftist parties over those of the right. In his Introduction Camus is chilling: "If murder has rational foundations, then our period and we ourselves are rationally consequent. If it has no rational foundations, then we are insane and there is no alternative but to find some justification or to avert our faces. It is incumbent upon us, at all events, to give a definite answer to the question implicit in the blood and strife of this century" [*The Rebel*, trans. Anthony Bower (New York: Vintage Books, 1956), p. 4; *L'homme révolté* (Éditions Gallimard, 1951), pp. 16-17].

The state-sponsored murder we refer to as a burnt sacrifice (Holocaust) had and continues to have rational foundations. Murder, although not acknowledged as such, has become reasonable. Humaneness and innocence are now naive assumptions of those already judged guilty of not promoting the proper cause. More than ever before, people stand today in anticipation of death, that which Heidegger took as the possibility of authentic existence.

Auschwitz and the world into which we have been "thrown" by its intensifying whirlwind, the world in which we all face the probability of inappropriate death, is not a world of insane inmates. It is a world to which we have been assigned and committed after having been found guilty, a world ruled by functionaries programmed with totalizing and unforgiving concepts. In this world of terror the best status is that of nominal innocence, that is, the presumption of innocence *until* (not unless) proven guilty. We have no choice. We must face the judges and the philosophies that render their death sentences rational. This is the theme/dilemma of Jean-François Lyotard's *Le Différend* (1983).

Today, more than Hegel and Marx, even more than Kierkegaard, Heidegger confronts us as both thinker-judge and potential liberator. It is this tension and vacillating ambiguity of Heidegger's texts that must be *read* against both those who idolize him as judge and those who want to destroy him as thinker. That which flies over the cuckoo's nest is not the god of the judges.

In a series of lectures written and presented at the same time that Camus' *L'homme Révolté* appeared, Heidegger ruled on the question of thinking. Whereas Camus says it is incumbent upon us to give a definite answer to the question concerning the rational foundations of state-sponsored murder, Heidegger says: "We *are capable* of thinking only insofar as we *are* endowed with what is most thought-provoking, gifted with what ever and always wants to be thought about . . . . It could be that we incline too slightly and too rarely to let ourselves become so involved. And that is so not because we are all too indolent, or occupied with other matters and disinclined to think, but because the involvement with thought is in itself a rare thing, reserved for few people" [*What Is Called Thinking?*, trans. Fred D. Wieck and J. Glenn Gray (New York: Harper & Row, 1968), p. 126; *Was Heisst Denken?*, 3rd Edition (Tübingen: Max Niemeyer, 1971), p. 86].

Camus addresses his readers, whereas Heidegger seductively appeals to that elitism which always needs to serve state powers: thinking is reserved for a few people who are endowed with what is most thought-provoking. How does one know if one if so endowed? It seems to have something to do with whether or not one is interested in and concerned with what is common: "What we encounter at first is never what is near, but always only what is common. It possesses the unearthly power to break us of the habit of abiding in what is essential, often so definitively that we never come to abide anywhere" (*What Is Called Thinking?*, p. 129). That which is most thought-provoking, the endowment of the few, is opposed to the unearthly power that keeps us from what is essential. Over and over Heidegger never tires of referring to "what is essential" *(Wesenhaften)*. Thinkers only think one (essential) thought and, thus, resist the unearthly power behind the plurality of readings which Heidegger calls the literature industry: "Literature is what has been literally written down, and copied, with the intent that it be available to a reading public. In that way, literature becomes the object of widely diverging interests, which in turn are once more stimulated by means of literature—through literary criticism and promotion" (*What Is Called Thinking?*, p. 134).

In 1966 Heidegger would repeat his "criticism" of popular or common literature. This time, however, he gives the grounds for his harsh judgment: "From our human experience and history, at least as far as I am informed, I know that everything essential and great has only emerged when human beings had a home and were rooted in a tradition. Today's literature is, for instance, largely destructive" ["Der Spiegel Interview" in *Martin Heidegger and National Socialism: Questions and Answers*, eds. Günther Neske and Emil Kettering (New York: Paragon House, 1990), p. 56]. Later in the interview these references to home (Heimat) and rootedness are made even clearer when Heidegger asserts that in the task of developing a free relationship to technology, "National Socialism went in that direction, [but] those people were much too limited in their thinking to gain a really explicit relationship to what is happening today and what has been under way for three centuries" ("Der Spiegel Interview," p. 61). That Heidegger could say this and no more about it in 1966 indicates the depth of his commitment to the "essential." It also indicates, of course, the extreme danger of such a resolute turning away from the common graves of those who experienced the consequences of "limited" thinking. On the importance of what Heidegger calls thinking and his failure to do it, see my "Why Heidegger Was Not Shocked By The Holocaust," *History of European Ideas*, 14/4 (1992).

What we find in Heidegger is a nostalgic post-modernism, a longing for access to Being through its contemporary traces and debris. To the best of my knowledge, the best discussion of this is Gianni Vattimo, *The End of Modernity: Nihilism and Hermeneutics in Postmodern Culture*, translated by Jon R. Snyder (Baltimore: John Hopkins University Press, 1988). However, my contention that the death camps changed everything by creating a radical separation of the tradition from our mutated and impaired existence is quite different than Heidegger's claim that the *Ge-stell* announces the event of Being in the modern age of global technology (see Vattimo, p. 41). For Heidegger, the death camps and their destruction processes do not constitute a transformative event. This, however, does not place Heidegger outside of the transformation. Quite the contrary. There is with Heidegger and his texts, or I should say with the many Heideggers and their many texts, a struggle with the complicity and implications of *Ge-stell*. A very far-reaching and necessarily complex treatment of this involvement is found in Avital Ronell's *The Telephone Book: Technology, Schizophrenia, Electric Speech* (Lincoln: University of Nebraska Press, 1989).

The stance taken in this preface is very close to that of Theodore Adorno's *Negative Dialectics* and to that of Jean-François Lyotard's reading of Adorno [*Heidegger and "the jews,"* trans. Andreas Michel and Mark Roberts (Minneapolis: University of Minnesota Press, 1990), Chapters 13 and 14]. At the same time that Heidegger gave his *Der Spiegel* interview, Adorno wrote: "There is no Being without entities. 'Something'—as a cogitatively indispensable substrate of any concept, including the concept of Being—is the utmost abstraction of the subject-matter that is not identical with thinking, an abstraction not to be abolished by any further thought process. Without 'something' there is no thinkable formal logic, and there is no way to cleanse this logic of its metalogical rudiment. The supposition of an absolute form, of 'subject-matter at large' that might enable our thinking to shake off that subject-matter, is illusionary" [*Negative Dialectics*, trans. E. B.

Ashton (New York: The Seabury Press, 1973), p. 135]. The danger of this illusion is nowhere more apparent and menacing than in the case of the death camps and attempts to think them away with traditional concepts. This is, I believe, exactly what Heidegger attempted to do when he displaced the transformative event of the death camps under the sway of the forgetfulness of Being.

What is "profoundly" lacking in Heidegger is any sense of the sense-giving of rebellion. But what Heidegger lacks can be supplied by a solidarity that refuses to kill the judge on the same grounds that the judge uses to pass sentence: "Man's solidarity is founded upon rebellion, and rebellion, in its turn, can only find its justification in this solidarity. We have, then, the right to say that any rebellion which claims the right to deny or destroy this solidarity loses simultaneously its right to be called rebellion and becomes in reality an acquiescence in murder"—*The Rebel*, p. 22. The massive mutating trauma which we are has no access to any Being other than all those who have already stood before the judges and refused to accept their sentences—"guilty." The judges have always been plagued by the likes of Zoyd Wheeler, who refuses to take his own life not because the world of the judges has any significance, but rather because whatever is left of significance comes from defying them: "Only thing that holds me back," Zoyd blowing his nose at length, "is the indignity of lying there all splattered by the pool and in my last few seconds on Earth hearing Jack Lord say, 'Book him, Danno—Suicide One'" [Thomas Pynchon, *Vineland* (Boston: Little, Brown and Company, 1990), p. 60]. Camus would have imagined Zoyd as happy as Sisyphus.

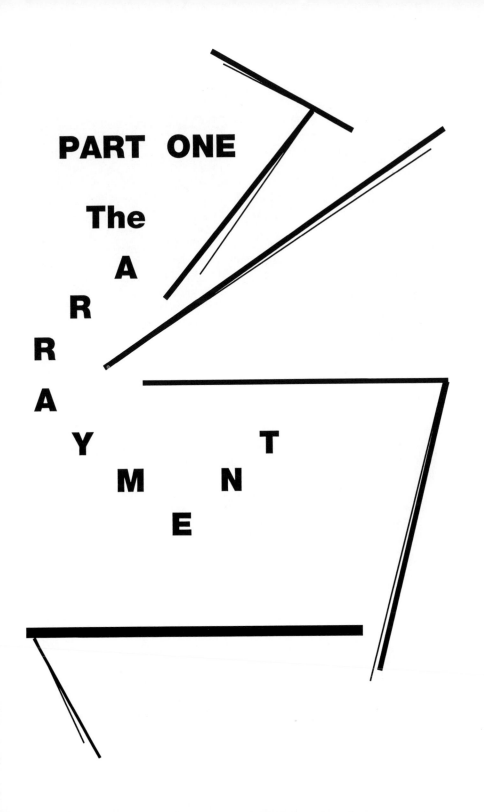

PART ONE

The

A
R
R
A
Y
M   E   N
T

28

Surface Tensions

facet 1
semiterate writing

Writers desire to be seductive, to successfully lure their readers into textual effects. Philosophical writing-seduction is a species of misleading, one which supposedly moves from appearances to what is real and true. But philosophers are perpetually frustrated seducers. Every promising lead to the real and true is always nothing but appearances. The seduction lies in the apparent sincerity of promises and the severity of well-staged struggles with anti-real forces. Reading and writing within this metaphysical framework are non-playful and lead only to the frustration of delayed gratification, with occasional fits of revolutionary passion. Unless, that is, readers and writers mingle promiscuously in the never ending foreplay of post-philosophical discourse. Such is the perversity that never sours on texts and refuses to burn books in the fires of *ressentiment*.

For the post-philosophical writer-reader, there is no final or definitive reading of texts, including philosophical texts, nor is there any hierarchy of texts. Philosophy and literature belong to idolaters only when their promising mis-leads have the temporary effect Plato warned about the many times he promised us the truth.

There is, however, a way of avoiding this philosophical mis-lead. Promiscuous reading-writing without benefit of genre organization becomes seductive in educing itself to its own appeal. In remembrance of Plato's *Phaedrus* and Socrates' ironic piety we will characterize this kind of post-metaphysical imaging of hierarchical images as eroscophic—always a way of seeing otherwise than the State closures and its death machines.

Actually the term "post-metaphysical" is misleading. There have always been readers-writers who side-stepped the hierarchies and the thoughts behind them. The term is useful, however, as an indicator of the dangers we all face—the appropriations called Good, Beauty, Truth, History (GOBETH). It would be as dangerously naive to believe that these appropriations do not exist as to say that GOBETH exists. Whatever exists does so contingently and specifically, and whenever some specific power is formed and set forth as other than contingent, it is always done so as an appropriation of GOBETH. The terms "post-metaphysical" and "eroscophic" are current redescriptions of what very cautious side-stepping and tip-toeing writers-readers have always done. When one reads-writes GOBETH otherwise than as an appropriation/property, caution is necessary because current configurations of power are extremely frustrated and deadly. From the perspective of such deadly intensity, eroscophic activity is per/sub/multi-versive narcissism. It is, in other words, the truth of their Truth—power is always a shifting contingency.

In a certain sense, and from a certain perspective, eroscophic activity is narcissistic. Yes, but the private has always been part of power configurations. Neither the private nor the public realm is seamless. Eroscophic writing-reading finds the ruptures in appropriations (GOBETH), and explores those regions by cautiously hanging onto the sides of these ruptures. Eroscophers fear what the appropriators relish—the abyss beneath all power. The abyss is the end of all seductive appeal. The depths beneath the articulated surfaces are infinite. Surfaces, including their split sides, appeal because they are limited, meaningful. Surfaces, never continuous, never completely smooth or safe, attract across an annihilating abyss. The pretended appropriation of truth is the denial of the danger of attraction.

Eroscophers gather from the flow and articulate as much as possible, just short of losing their grasp. Reaching into an abyss is not the same as either falling into it or leaping over it. We eroscophers are neither clumsy nor as nimble footed as those who in pursuit of the metaphysical mislead run and hop, dance, fly and motor their way across and beyond the limited surfaces. In its allegretto mode, eroscophical activity is a meandering of semi-illiteracy hoping to chance upon the failures of appropriated texts. But eroscophic activity can never offer plot, or any real depth, only themes, predicaments, struggles, and apparitions—all the things that prevent the closure of GOBETH. But no telos can be detected in these meanderings. Eroscophers are lovers who take too much time to worry about completion. There are no finalities, only pauses in the flow of the earth and its many voices.

Hegel, the great mediator, appropriated Plato and many others in what is now taught as the History of philosophy. But his appropriated Plato is no longer seductive. Hegel, good Christian that he was, felt compelled to offer his readers a good deal of assurance that a finality was finally on its way. Today Hegel tells people what they want to hear after they lose their grasp and fall into the abyss of appropriation. Eroscophers want to rescue as many as possible from this Truth-Death.

Nietzsche tells us that metaphysics is that schooling of the body called asceticism. For what? The truth, the whole truth! Hegel is the negation, *Aufhebung*, of love, seduction, of all fetishism. Marx was, after all, a great metaphysician.

the hell of subjectivity

Hell exists—such has been our insistence for so long now. And true to modern delusions of sovereignty, the abstract space and time of Subjectivity (modern appropriating thought's denial of contingency) came to Luther on the privy. Inscribed within epistemological texts penned in the certainty of salvation, the modern appropriation of desire to know and master everything has sources too deep and terrible for the all-knowing Subject we are supposed to have become. Instead of facing and resisting that appropriation, modern thought insists that all not yet known is dialectically other than itself.

Dialectically, as lust, the Subject is the same as its otherness, but not yet conjugated. The identity of Subject and Object is satiation, the End of Desire. In Hell everything is defined by this destructive act, the identity of identity and difference. The modern version of Hell exists; it is the dialectic of consumption and production. Economic life is the focal point of dialectics, the endlessness of which continually betrays the promise of finality. Hard work is so frustrating! And then the fall into the abyss of state-induced criminality.

The Subject—all consuming flame of desire, Hell-fire itself—is the subject–object Identical, the very fate of modern, self–made Man. With Him there arrives the idea of eternal revolution and eternal recurrence of need. Swollen to fantastic proportions, the Male Subject penetrates the Other and fills her unmediated void. Hell exists; it is the obscene presence of the Gap covered–over and over–filled with the flesh of labor–power. Yet the Gap remains the dominant principle. The Gap is the finality to be reached, seized, mediated, manipulated, conquered, possessed, subjected. Finally, the negation of the Negation.

But first, a little alienated fun. The inversion of the penetrated Gap, the productive principle, comes to the side of need. Self–generating and self–originating (in the dialectical sense), it then resurrects itself as a new election, better fitted to the demands of the consuming principle. The Gap becomes the inversion of the fulfilling principle—the Subject twisting around itself in a publicly flaunted autoerotic embrace. Greater consumption, eating itself, demands greater production. There is no free lunch in the self-formation of the Subject "mediating" its others. Pulsating, revolving, waxing and waning, appearing and disappearing, the Subject is the knowing of what it is doing—wildly, somehow! The whirlwind of epistemological subjects in the abyss of the state's rapture consumes everything hanging onto the sides of ruptures.

Everything is the Subject, the totality quite alone. "We" cannot see the Subject, which talks only to Himself in a great monologue of Being. He is the voice without difference, the inaudible utterance of suspended death, an inscription deeply etched in the self–sufficient text that needs no oration. The secret of ultimate penetration, the great cosmic rape, cannot be "grasped" by remainders—survivors. *Wieviel stücke* remaining?

But the cosmic eggshell of this mutilating Subject has been broken. Not by need or necessity, but by freely given responses in polyvocal dissonance. The identity of identity and difference is broken by kind-less eroticism, that aberrant sexuality which delights in the unmediated other. But we still have to tip-toe in the cracks of Being.

Does the Subject hear the voice and the touching in the cracks of its egg-Being? What/who could possibly break through the din of this hellish coupling with itself? The objectivity of subjective need keeps the Subject revolving around its own center of gravity. The Subject thus persists in His self–penetration, right down to His own universal zero–point, the Ego? Here, in this metaphysical *Abgrund*, we enter the realm of the suspended death called madness.

The Ego—all conquered territory, the nothing–but–subjection. The Ego makes nothing. He is made up of expropriations, and protects this booty against further theft. The Other is the other of this defensive-consuming Ego. Projected outward, as he appears, the other becomes Other only with momentary relaxations of His penetrating weapon. Thus modern epistemic cognition is strategic. The Other appears as that which has not yet been reduced to suspended death. The Other is outside of His text, the master narrative.

But is it really possible for semi-illiterates to make a good case against Hegel, his legacy and the forces of culture fueling it? Hegelian universality—the State—mediates everything. Is it still possible not to be led into the meta-physical mis–lead of this universality? These and other self-doubts as we hang from the sides of a ruptured and erupting master narrative. So contingent, so vulnerable that our self-doubting might fall into the service of the totality: suspended by threads of solidarity, enough solidity perhaps to mark the tracks of great leaps of desire in the master text.

Carnality, exposed flesh, unrelated, hanging together, marking the points of bound transcendence. But, schooled in ascetic mediation, the modern reader does not respond kindly to such remainders and reminders of the texts the master texts cover-up.

Unfamiliar with the cultural, historical, and physical materiality of the expressions which symbolically mediate the master text, the modern reader needs the violence of progress without residues. It is as if there were no desire to remember the moments of surrender, relaxations of defenses and weapons. Which is why semiterate writing is many styles, each and all of which frustrate those who have learned intolerance of traces, reminders, and limits.

the fine style

The more one wishes to be socially useful, the easier one will be understood by the collected and mediated Subject—the masses. There is a reciprocal sharing here, a give and take mediated very grammatically. To be well received requires a dedication to the Social: a matter of taste and decorum, this thing called the Social Question.

Morality acquires the silky lining of fine style when its angry types are converted to the dialectical needs of the masses. The revolutionary is a matter/master of taste in mass–thinking and acting. In the grammatically correct letter of the collected Subject, the revolutionary is a rebel become species–being. Can eroscophers rescue these rebels?

But even with the finest of styles, exquisitely tailored to mass needs and desires, idiosyncrasies can be found. No rebel-become-revolutionary has ever reached the stage of total species–being: as writer the revolutionary cannot attain the level of his Concept. He tries to improvise the little slips and accidents of his praxis, but the Concept judges him harshly. Consider how many corrections were necessary before even Marx could be regarded as socially useful. And when he became such, this eroscopher became a state program.Which, however, is the Marxian legacy?

Morality is the movement, perhaps dialectical in nature, of grammar. People become moral when they acquire proper sense combinations. Writing ungrammatically is a wrong against the subject-object Identical. We must be prudent as to where and how we place/have our copulates. The socially useful writer writes properly, i.e., anti-eroscophically. This is why all revolutions go after artists: revolution is always a matter of good taste— leaders.

Prudence would dictate that the semiterate appear literate when read by the well schooled. To do so, however, would force the semiterate to make allusions to transcendental warrants, especially those called the Good, whatever its current appropriation. At great risk, the semiterate writer sticks to surfaces, their sides and discontinuity, and thus hangs suspended between the fantastic antipodes of the master tradition's ruptures. Above all, semiterates cannot follow the mis–lead into the abyss. It is that mis–lead which metaphysicians lead others to while they themselves leap over it. Semiterate writing discloses that metaphysical cleverness and attempts to rescue readers from its mis-lead. Remember: there are limits to everything, including our ability to understand. Things can be addressed only by acknowledging limits. Limits keep us from falling, endlessly, in the abyss. Life is sustained by acknowledging vulnerability and protecting one another, but never by the Subject.

Since the great Aristotelian appropriation, the spirited part of human nature has been regarded as the part that must be subordinated to reason. Thus systematic philosophy, among other things, subdues the spirit. It does this, sometimes only temporarily, by seriality and organization, by logical and grammatically sound hierarchies of Being. When Being is talked about, the spirit is in its proper place. The spirit is like our best friends the dogs who want to play without leashes. But like the domesticated dogs, the spirit has been leashed. Held in check, the subdued spirit does not interrupt the thinker who feels compelled to finish things, to continue until the system is built and the totality formulated. Philosophy was unfinished until Hegel. After Hegel, it became a matter of method—mediation. The domesticated dog barks only upon command. The compulsion to finish is now just a matter of fitting things into their proper categories. Prison is the idea of law and order made real. Now, everything has its place, especially the things that don't fit. The strong sense of disjunction is weak after all.

Is there a prison for texts that don't fit, that read interminably? Do schooled readers police such texts and their readers? Is the university a place of higher learning? Is the mind opened by the insistence that it complete everything it undertakes to understand? Discipline! Is it completed things that we see? Camus answers: "If the world were clear, art would not exist." Why do revolutionaries go after the artists? Methodology—ideology: the mediating Subject in search of Self. What is our eroscophical narcissism compared with this?

Self–exposure

sur-faces

Shifting imagings of the impenetrable depths, outward and inward, surfaces present the senses with uncensored articulations of emerging qualities. Appearances are shameless. Censorship begins with the introduction of shame to the flowing, gathering eruption of things. Attempts to probe beneath the abundance of things, coeval with the beginnings of philosophy, have their origin in the distraction created by surfaces drawing apart from one another. Human beings dwell in the separating of surfaces. More so than those preceding him, Plato seductively has old Socrates resolutely lose his grip. He thus abandons protean beings caught in the limits–shifts of the earth's flow in favor of the metaphysical mis–lead into the abyss. We learn from this Socrates that the danger to the taut suspension of human dwelling is rigidity, especially the rigid insistence on probity. Like its counterpart, probity breaks the fragile thread holding us toward the abyss. We have learned that walking upright is not always wise. Let us then leave probing to those who cannot lie on occasion.

There are beings that crawl, wiggle, climb, burrow, and fly. With the exception of flying, we share in this community of activity. Probity is grounded in a profound dissatisfaction with the human condition. The fear of flying is well grounded, and the desire to soar is well founded. Often forgotten: a leap is alright only when it soars over what has already been stumbled upon. *Laufen—lauhen:* the leaper is praised only after another has stumbled. On the same footing, if one stoops, one runs the risk of becoming a stump/step for another's stamp.

On a busy walkway, a boy suddenly stops and stoops to examine a stone frozen in the concrete. Eyes fastened on her destination, a well–dressed woman stumbles over the stooping boy. A third, in contemporary attire and very alert, leaps over both boy and woman without losing a stride. Was Zarathustra bent over when he proclaimed that all life was a matter of taste? Let's ask this question scientifically, but also in the manner of the eroscophic Nietzsche.

perspectives

Position A:	At 90 degrees to two bodies approaching one another. One body is dark and small. The other is large and light–emitting.
Observation:	The closer the dark body gets to the larger body, the brighter the dark body becomes.
Position B:	Now located directly behind the smaller, dark body.
Observation:	The bright, light–emitting body becomes blotchy, sickly looking.

Scientific Refinements of the Observations

1. Never stand directly behind or in front of a scholar who is explaining a great thinker.
2. Primary sources eventually destroy whatever they shed light upon, unless the latter keeps its proper distance.
3. Interpretations are dangerous when the interpreters seem to occupy privileged points of view.
4. There is a sound physical and spiritual reason for the advised use of sunglasses.
5. There are some blemishes which only seem to appear on the surface of great bodies.

Semiterate writing simply cannot do without stumbling, leaping, and stooping. Nor can it do without a laugh or two. The unschooled, erotic reader knows that every text is filled with stumps. Literate writers number these stumps and use them as a device called the footnote—a very sly form of appropriation. In semiterate writing these stumps are unnumbered and occur everywhere in the text. The stumps of the text are the situs of the legacy of authors, the places where the writer falls silent as stone.

Like the silence in all great music, the unnumbered stumps evoke a muse that draws us to something. The footing of any text is not easy to track, especially when it is numbered. Perhaps this is because the writer can only be a pedate who teaches through the text and its stumps out of love for the stooped and falling.

to be a man[ager]

According to the veritable tradition of masculinity, to be a man is to seemingly overcome the vulnerability of one's biological inheritance. "You gotta have balls!" is the slogan, as well as an expression of unadulterated biological fatalism. Within the scope of this tradition, balls are the limit point of masculine consciousness. To protect one's "equipment" (method)— this is the telos of the master narrative.

Biological reasoning has it that female security stems from the innermost sanctity of the ovaries as compared to the external vulnerability of male genitalia. On this "basis" arises, fully erect, the system of symbolic domination in praise of nature's wisdom.

Male consciousness is a symptom displayed in dialectics. The "play" of opposites: vulnerability becomes dominance through modes of assertion, negation, reversal, and mastery. The game is symbolism, the phallus, the autonomous self–asserting Subject in the face of all threats to its equipment. You gotta have balls to play this symbolic thrust of the phallus. No metaphors limping here!

A paralyzing fear turned into a cocky assurance of domination. A mean little feat of no great complexity, but nonetheless a feat . . . and very mean. Much of what passes for history and progress revolves in this little simplicity of dialectical opposites playing with and in themselves.

The tradition has it that only vis-à-vis the streamlined female figure can the flaccid male member become seemly, erect and less comical than in its non-dominant solitary state. Yet, since the fall from grace of the Thomistic-Aristotelian idea of the male formative principle, the role of the male has become marginal in biological reproduction. But the marginal compensates by moving to center stage, a move which has had a very high price, aesthetically speaking. Thrusting onto center stage takes place in the realm of the imagination: phallocentrism is never creative but always wildly imaginative. For the male–member–Subject everything rises and falls when kicked in its center. Aesthetics recenters the male principle of biological texts. The Nazis understood the significance of this shift.

One wonders just how far this imaginary has carried us out of real history— female speculation, no doubt. Are women to be feared because they are indeed superabundant and secure? Is it only men who need to be what they lack? Tradition would prompt us to say that all goals are representations of what is not yet present. But, perhaps, all symbolism is compensation for the imaginary rather than representation of what is not present.

Human–nature: a taut bow with neither arrow nor target, a female–male convolution. Within the orbit of the male imaginary, this convolution is seen as revolutionary, a turning over and around. For women the question becomes what to do with men who see themselves in the eternal orbit of their imaginary power to negate the convolution.

Biologically, the human is feman. Differentiation of the convolution is symbolic and rebellious, both functions of the convolution itself. Dialectical thinking attempts to co-opt the convolution; it is a centering that symbolically masculates all differentiations. Thus, the identification of authors, founders, creators—each and every one a Father. The Other is the repudiation of this masculating center.

Semiterate writing de-identifies from the inside to the outside; it is the words that delimit the writer and bind her to the Other he has become. I become myself in the imaging of the convolution. Surpassing monologue, advanced narcissism, the mirror of sovereignty and the play of auto-eroticism, self–other consciousness trembles with the vulnerability and responsibility it has become. Its enemy is the subject–object Identical and its imaginative variations.

Kelly s Heroes

facet 2
monotheistic compulsion

Belief strengthens as the illusion of reference to what one believes in bears fruit. And the powers which bring these fruits are strengthened as the illusion of reference is naturalized as it by-passes their fruit-bringing operations. "Yes, Virginia," says daddy, "there is a Santa Claus." Why disillusion the child? Language is not a game!

Believers in the One, True God do not leave things unfinished. Most of the great thinkers were nurtured in the monotheistic discipline. They all developed the compulsion for finishing and totalizing. Even if one didn't believe, it was necessary to wear this mask in order to be recognized. Thus all completed work became a mark of mastery and a mask the fruit bringers insisted upon. The mark of mastery was bestowed when one completed a system of thought that reiterated the great chain of created being. Everything complete crossed-over gaps with faith and belief in the perfectibility of the created order of things. In time everything would be revealed to the faithful mind. Strong belief, the fundament of monotheistic culture, was the masking of these gaps.

One of these gaps was disbelief. Against the fundament, the many silences of writing announced unmasked and incomplete "authors." Polyphonic discord, the writing of difference, became the target of something called "authorship." Authorship is the authority of rewriting, filling-in the gaps with one voice. The consummate skill of faithful and loyal authors brought texts to completion in works/books just as The Book of many authors was rewritten to completion.

Together with the technical interpretation of thinking as logic, ordered sequence, the mask of authorship is a technical achievement linking incomplete texts with technically accomplished actors. If the illusionary power of the latter is great enough, the incomplete texts appear as completed works. Nothing changes in this game when the author–actor is plural. Behind every collective there is one voice of authority. This is the mask demanded by the fruit bringers.

To unmask this culture and its totalizing belief, it is sufficient to show that the appearance of completed works conceals an ascetic despotism. If

Daddy insists on Santa Claus and the reverent Fathers on God, we could test that insistence on referential veracity by calling forth, for example, Frank Miller's "Batman" and M. L. Ciccone's "Madonna"—two challenges to the univocal Law of the Father. But it is also necessary to show, as Derrida does, the "abysmation" of the masked master text.

Educated with the monotheistic culture machine, our senses have become mediators. They tend toward completed perception with a minimum of clues. Always on the alert, modern bourgeois sensibility reads–off and away the very materiality of texts. Baudrillard arises and despairs. But this "modern materialism" has nothing to do with the abundance of polyphonic nature–human. The more one reads, the more sources resound in polyvocal dissonance. But that troubles our mediated senses and our need for the one true bringers of fruits. Just as we are about to transfer allegiance to a new god, she winks at us. Yes, we are modern and postmodern simultaneously.

spiritual consumption

There are miserable, stinking slicks of consuming flesh inscribing their filth on every surface of the tortured earth. The earth's innards are not spared, not even the furthest reaches of its aura. The pigs have not inherited the earth, rather they have submitted it to the etchings of their own abstract bowels—the asceticized spirit.

We must ask: are these pigs caricatures of the earth? Everywhere, they consume and inscribe the Truth on everything partial, incomplete, ambiguous. They are bodies with taut organs in pursuit of the Lack.

The aim of the slave today, the bourgeois Subject, is to become a flow of shit—a kind of transcendent defecation or paralogism in action. What can we do but watch and taste . . . we, the ones with the mouths and anuses of the earth.

Is it possible to make a mark without a big, erect organ? Is there just one true carrier of meaning? Is the earth without wisdom because it is so many? Must we continue to drink the imaginary? How have we been taught to see and think?

Imperious Self-Doubt

the logic of monotheism

It is really quite simple. As all that is, the One is nothing but Power. Thus it created and entered into relations with its creations: its identity became relational, but no less Almighty. To kill off a part or two changed nothing essential. But just as a part was nothing in itself to the relational identity, parts shared the relational One's identity. Some parts thus attempted to become the pre-creational One, the Almighty in itself. The One had become a mirror identity, which is to say, reflective.

The knowledge of relations was reflected in mirror identity , and with this came the knowledge of good and evil. The reflected was good, and the reflector evil . . . because it was somehow not relational. It was precisely the non-sovereignty of the reflector, its incredible opacity, that defied all relationship with the Almighty. Power saw itself in and by means of the reflector, but it could not see the reflector. There was something there; the One knew this much because there was something, something very troubling that did not assimilate. That something did not and could not reflect its assigned identity. This opaque unassimilable thing was rebellious, absurd.

What had happened was that the imaginaries of the Almighty had fallen upon things: pure mind had come to matter.

In the beginning was the word. But when it resounded, the echo had a resonance. The secondary vibrations had a source other than the beginning. Such was the case with human beings, all resounding in secondary modes. Thus began the quest for the primary mode, the return to the beginning, to the imaginary without opposition. The limits of the absurd became unbearable for the human creatures. They longed for a release from absurdity, from secondary resoundings. Theirs was the dream of imaginary sovereignty, freedom from matter, embodiment. Humans longed for the Lack and they pursued it by learning good and evil. This was the beginning of theological education.

What was desired was Nothing, the pure state of Being. Humans began to dream the Nothing with its companion, the Imaginary. Dreaming aspired to the relational, non-existential identity of Being and Nothing. The world of their dreams was perfectly clear, and its transparency offered the imaginary no resistance, no reflections. Dreaming this way, humans did not think anything. But the Almighty could now dream only because it had entered into relation with secondary vibrations. The Nothing was blocked for the Almighty. For human beings, on the other hand, the Almighty blocked nothing. Each dreamer heard his dreams come back fulfilled exactly as desired.

It did not seem quite right. Having met matter, the Sovereign had fallen into limitation while its creations, images, were dreaming Sovereignty for themselves. But when the imaging images of the dreamers met one another, it seemed that not all could be sovereign. This was resisted and sovereignty was turned into a graven image, an idol. In his heart (heard over and over by the Almighty), each man knew he was right. So transfixed by their graven images, humans began the war against one anothers' idols.

Graven images do not image; they are things frozen at an imaginary end–point. One cannot see in a graven image anything but the graven image; they do not elicit interpretation, transformation, undoing. Idols were the beginning of fixed ideas, essences. Philosophy originated with the great theological wars of idols against idols. From its inception, philosophy allied itself with the violence of essences. Philosophy was to become the quest for the Truth, the essence so graven that it could be seen only with the mind. Philosophy was the Sovereign's last happy dream, and theology's mutation.

In this new dream state it was clear that the rule of the One was the only possible true organization of men. The knowledge of good and evil had finally come upon its goal, and with this the logic of human sovereignty was born. Within this imaginary event the Sovereign knew that it would be unnecessary to become one of its creations. It would be sufficient to simply redream it, over and over.

Papa's Sermon

gravity and the real

On earth the Unitary was coming in at magnitude seven. Mars came in with five, and Venus with a six. The earth's moon, defying all known laws, was computing a very disturbing thirty-three. But, then, Jupiter surprised everyone by disclosing a one. Still, it was not a steady state one.

They watched for the flicker. Sure enough, it came after three revolutions. The One flickered and reappeared in nine sections. Reality was One, but not yet a steady One. The Unitary was still pulsing.

At the edge of the black hole, the Unitary was pulsing at thirty-three times its Jovian rate. Near the center the pulse rate was the speed of light minus One. A theory was proposed: at the center of the Nothing, the Unitary is steady state, or infinite pulsation of multiple Ones in any one time–space event. The One contains itself in the moments of infinite multiplication, but only if the gravity of the moment events equals the greatest possible mass. Thus the One and the absolutely homogeneous event are Identical. Neither exist since they are Real. Simply put: real things do not exist.

Against the standard of the Real, the Unitary, the multiplicity of existence does not count. It is the spirit of gravity that weighs matters. The ashes don't really matter in the metaphysical-scientific scheme of "things."

Four thousand years before all of this, the same results were reached. The gods of Olympias affirmed the multiplicity of existence at 12,000 feet above sea level. In exactly the same time-event, Plato and Aristotle went down to the Unitary that was then pulsing at sea level—every seven seconds, to be exact.

All surfaces and artifices are attacked by the monotheistic imaginary—the spirit of gravity and the not-to-be-fooled-with logic of sovereignty. The abyss widens, but appears everywhere as an amalgamation of surfaces. So, for the disillusioned wide-ranging celebrant of superficiality, the depths have become unavoidable. Even the sound fear that kept us from previously over-reaching ourselves is now impotent against the omnipresent depths.

Profundity is the achievement of shallow thinkers, those who turned out poorly. Shallow is the thinking which reaches so deeply with categories so high. Essence, unity, soul, truth, substance—all figments of the imaginary against playful superficiality. Their words are set forth in stone, graven, do not image in their appropriation of imaging.

What lies beneath the cracked surfaces of the world are traces of the murderous processes that stripped the flesh from peoples, twisted their bodies so hideously that they had only "souls" left. Everything transcendental has this violent origin. The furnaces of hell are stoked with earthly flesh. The transcendent ones reached down to hell to save the burning ones, but their pale categories only reached out to their smoking souls. Then it was clear: not a failure of reach, but a necessary disembodiment. The bodies burned so that the souls could be liberated from superficiality. This was the purification of the world. The imaginary tolerates no resistance. Is it possible to bear these wounds without madness? Are we lovers of superficiality strong enough for an archeology of the deadly, vengeful knowledge we carry about and within us?

the abyss

The journey downward into the hell of resentment and revenge brings terrible sounds to our ears, still open to sounds. The abundance of our reserves is soon exhausted. How much further must we drop before the ugliness of these sounds consumes us? It seems almost necessary to leave our superficiality behind, to begin to take nourishment from all this ugliness in order to keep descending, but . . .

The stench! It is too much for humans to endure. What sovereign demands this much sacrifice? Haven't we embraced it, worshipped it, fought for it, humbled ourselves for it? The stench, the sounds, too much, and the sacrifices aren't yet visible.

We remember the surface, the sun, the play of color and musical life. Not true, we are remembering something that does not exist. The earth has become the imaginary. We must continue. There is no return to what never existed.

The infernal smoke is transforming us. We know this about ourselves. Nothing needs to be said about the power of the dark ugly dirtiness enveloping us.

Batline

The level of silence is finally reached. Here the sounds of the ugly are deafening, but we are now attuned. Fascinated by this powerful ugliness, the time for hesitation passes us by . . . for good.

Ugliness, no longer separate from us, we turn inward. The smell of the burning flesh spurs our spiritual juices. Never have we felt more real. We stand riveted to the force of the ugly, the cacophony of pain and suffering has true significance. Our eyes have been opened to the deeper real meaning of things. The inhuman is human! We see clearly. There is no contradiction, there is no play of differences now. Finally, we have come upon an understanding of the profundity of dialectics. The depths are really the surface. Our journey has been a spiritual one!

There is a discipline–compulsion riveting us to the face of the abyss, and now we understand this necessity. Energy, previously suppressed, pours forth into the power of ugliness. But our transformation is still incomplete for we are still ashamed that we cannot turn away in horror and revulsion. Yet the abyss draws us deeper, more profoundly. How far? Are there no limits to human suffering? The stench is stronger. Then we see the burning children. The flesh of the future is burning. But we know our souls are getting stronger, more pure, so to speak.

Suddenly, a fool cried out, "Who is responsible for this atrocity?" The rest of us turn and see that her revulsion is mixed with fascination. We all share this fascination, but it is mixed with that bodily hanger-on, shame. Turned away from one another we recognize that the abyss draws proportionately to our own denial of limits. Limits versus power. Can power be proportionate? Is there any way to stop the transcendence of limits? Our souls protest these questions.

But our fascination with the abyss and its purifying flames erases these questions, this remembrance of things past. Here, we resolve, there are no limits, only fascination and the unrestrained imaginary of the spirit. Heaven/Hell—the denial of limits—this is the assurance of a spirit, now ours, which knows no bounds. The flesh burns so that the spirit can live! No longer are we touched by the earth. In the divine–demonic romance of human sacrifice there are only infinite capacities. Ours, all ours, finally. The Other holding us back from our due is finally sacrificed. Promise—sacrifice—undergoing and remaining decent—fulfillment. The Holocaust.

But then her hand touched mine.

The imaginary was shattered. Neither of us cried; we were rescued from the world without limits. In the abyss, we saw what has become of our surfaces. Our spiritual journey was shattered with the recognition that we never left the surface.

The decimation of humanity is horizontal, and it on this plane that the disillusioned decide to stay—without transcendental warrants, without soul, without spirit. Their imaginary has been shattered. Instead of soul, what remains for them is remembrance of what was within them, what made them complicitous with the powers of death.

We have seen man and profundity; we have seen his depths. We have seen the basis of his idealism, and we have felt the primal impulse of civilization. We know why he has turned out so badly. We remember the burning children. The leap of the imaginary is not necessary for those who can still dance and mourn. We experienced horror without subjection to the powers producing it. The foundation, the depths, no longer subject us but only those who remain silent. Those who do not remember in the trance of fascination are the spiritual ones waiting for the next exigency of their soul. All transcendence is crossed-out by the suffering of the children.

Remembrance: to keep the burnt children on the surface.

The Phenomenon of the World: deformity.

Plurality and Beauty: the disappearance of Sovereignty.

premature transformation

There is as much spirituality as forgetfulness. Many still want us to keep the burning future in the depths of the spirit. But forgetfulness and vengeance against the play of surfaces keeps us from facing the deformity which we and our world have become. Forgetfulness, the unconscious factory of spirituality, pulls us into its depths, as if the deformity lay there rather than on the surface. We must, say the spiritual ones, become better people, more moral, more spiritual. From the depths, a call comes from that "good" which always announces itself only after the atrocities. Then, "responding," come the old tests and trials of purification.

But forgetting and "responding" to the call of conscience (the "good") are further deformations of the world deformed by the disaster. Yes, we have been deformed by the burnt children and displacing this deformation carries on the legacy of deformation. Forgetting and becoming spiritual is the new idealism of the old "purification." Imagine: a childrens' park transforming

Deconstruction

Birkenau into a scene of innocent play. Such is the pull of unbound
transcendence. The Nazis were idealists who understood our soul.

Thinking is moved by something irrepressible. For earth–bound thinkers
this is the deformity of our world. Jewish children were burnt alive because
it would have cost more to gas them. They perished because the innocence
of their birth condemned them to idealist standards. More precisely, they,
like their parents, were murdered because they were innocent. As a people
the Jews had steadfastly refused salvation. They would not acknowledge
Jesus as the Christ–Savior. Innocent, they did not regard the earth as theirs
to possess and ravish. It was not enough that their innocence be falsified by
conspiracy fabrications, it became necessary to eradicate them as a people.
Even this was not enough for those with transcendental warrants: the
memory of their innocent existence and traditions had to be expunged from
human memory. To be "good," one must first murder. The new hermeneutic requires guilt followed by a flaming retreat from the world.

What is today irrepressible is this legacy of Nazi terrorism. There is a
terrifying linkage between Nazi racial anti-semitism and Christian theological anti-semitism; it is what I call "monotheistic compulsion." The terror of
this linkage is experienced when the thinker feels that compulsion in the face
of the world's deformity. Thinking still shares more with the murderers than
it does with the victims.

Does that about sum it all up? Isn't a completed text(book) always ugly until
it becomes an idol of our will to believe?

Materialized Idealism

facet 3
the idealism of economic separation

Weaving itself into the master narrative, capitalism brought to center stage the logic of peripheral exchange. Economics, the resultant science of this inversion, became the legitimating defense against all remaining externalities and anomalous marginalities. As a movement from the margins to the center, rendering everything exchangeable for the sake of exchange, capitalism displaced the family-centered business, replacing it with private firms from which all nonproductive functions had been eliminated. Social life contracted into a sphere of nonproductive relations as the privatized sphere of productive relations expanded. Progressively, the public space of work and collective norms were displaced by the privatization of production within firms and the subjection of workers to wage labor. Generated by the dominance of this privatized space of subjection, the social lives of labor and capitalists became separate and unequal. Capital and its proponents would thus speak of the common good in terms of this widening gap and the resultant superiority of the apparatus creating the gap.

A strange form of appearance is created by this movement of exchange from margin to center and its progressive social separation of worker and employer. The specter of work in the image of the subjected and isolated worker body is a strange image that looks quite different from its capitalist representation—the liberated wage laborer. Now defined by the ownership, control, and logic of scientific–technological production, the laboring body will become an increasingly abstract capitalist representation as it becomes more and more wretched in the space of its separated social life. This is the separation and its labor specter which Marx saw as a dialectical process of social development, a movement toward the abolition of private productive property and the development of worker class–consciousness. What was essential, as Marx saw it, was that the subjected worker perceive her subjection as a socializing process leading to the Subject–Object Identical of fulfilled time, the Future. But by accepting the separation and its privatizing generator, Marx prefigured that Marxism which would eventually become the ideology of capitalism's dialectical-logical movement. Thus Marxism became the idealism of capitalism and the leading spokesman of a metaphysical vision: the Becoming Visible of Species Freedom within the gap.

first dissemblance
the capitaliste style

Who were the artists that created machines? And who were the first artists to organize themselves into collective efforts to combine their machines, to link them together on one large, continually expanding canvas of the mind? Who were these experimental artistes?

They overcame the spell cast earlier by the priests and divine monarchs. They captured the masses set free by their own preliminary experiments with machines.

Who were these "herd artistes" that led the flocks in ways that put the old priests to shame?

An illusion—the mechanism—so powerful that it transformed its own creators into a play of created forces. The priests had never created anything so powerful, so exterior; they had until then remained within while above the religious life they organized, regulated, and administered. For the old priests, illusions were interior things. Only later would they become the atheists separate from what they set-up and administered.

Experimental in the most radical sense, each segment of the mechanism is now free to release its own forces, adding strokes to the expanding canvas. Each shape, color, line, and texture moving, blending, tracing something new but yet old. The canvas is painting itself. Automation— the only canvas on which the pigments never dry. There are no painters, only the painting. Supreme praxis!

We are machines, self-winding mechanisms of a Weltgeist in a perpetual self-expansion and contraction of great springs. Interlocking, interchanging, intercoursing parts. Great replaceables according to the needs of the painting. We are subjected to the fatigue of metal.

But then a new alloy, a new play of forces, a new mechanism, a new configuration, a rapidly expanding canvas. From this semblance we cannot extricate ourselves without adding a new stroke to the canvas.

Industrial democracy: a brush in every hand.

Only in America

The fabrication of generalized privacy is a semblance of the forceful subjugation of work to serialized labor. No one is "alone" any longer. Privacy has been spectered. Social life becomes generalized privacy and subjection, mere semblances on the intertextual canvas of economic exchange, semblances now taken for public appearances. The canvas painting itself becomes a delusional grid of mirror images of subjection, each reproducing the other in a discursive loop of interweavings.

The reduction of all appearance to economic semblance is the technified logic of organized violence. Thus, the cash nexus "appears" as the public manifestation of generalized private interests. Within this delusional grid, what is other cannot disclose the open realm of human appearance. Generalized privacy, in other words, occludes the artistic transformation which first disclosed the possibility of the cash nexus. It is as if the projection of the disclosure became independent of its supporting layers. The system of the disclosure becomes a delusional isolation from its points of disclosure. The depths of this delusional isolation are boundless. Thus, nihilism and the endless loop of discursive probings in pursuit of origins.

second dissemblance
the origin of the public

The private? Yes, indeed! From dreams and anarchy comes eventually the more permanent things of the public space. Attic tragedy transformed the private tribal member into a symbolic representative of the public individual. With feet of clay, this symbolic representative pointed to a way both beyond necessity and to the necessity of returning to necessity. Beyond father and mother, family, tribe, even beyond the private in general to the realm of sheer human togetherness, the public.

This theater of the emerging human world was and is a qualitative leap. Neither its origin nor its movement can be logically reconstructed. Reconstruction always serves the power of the established. A spectered publicity by private firms is not the same as the public space of appearance. Whenever the former is legitimated, transcendental warrants abound. Contingent beings can establish relatively permanent things, but the ever-unchanging things of eternity are not for mortals. Unbound transcendence should always make us suspicious of its complicity in making something earthly otherwise.

Established orders oppose transformations, and with best intensity, they war with those transformations they set into motion but cannot control. Which is why the power of transformative art has always seemed beyond us, in the Other (of the established realm).

With the transformation of the "species–being" into the world of plurality, ideas, deeds, and free play, the "necessity" of privatized being is temporally and partially suspended. Yet, freedom and equality, the distinctively human realm, are only as permanent as the artifices which create them. The possibility of human freedom lies in the difference between human being and being spectered. But privacy, whatever its form, is never surpassed by the public space of appearance. What appears in public began in privacy. Some day capitalism will appear in public.

Some day! Yes, after a long series of rebellions, each of which makes a segment of the monster appear. The beast is, however, polymorphic: whenever it gets "pictured," it changes form. But there is a constancy in this, one which it gets from the public space of appearance itself. In all of its various forms industrialism remains a movement against the public world in which it appears. Industrialism is iconoclastic polymorphic privacy committed to spectering in opposition to imaging. It is driven by an intense desire to "naturalize" everything, to establish "necessity," and to always revive tribal organizations for the subjected.

Industrialism is, in other words, a delusional primitivism attempting to transport its regressive idolatry into the public space without which it cannot appear. The beast attempts to appear against the very powers that makes its appearance possible. Polymorphic perversity always wants to control appearances from its private anti-political side of privilege. Yet it has no power of its own to do so, except for a power derived from the inevitable transformation of the public space whenever anything private appears there. The "space" of the visible manifestation of industrialism thus transforms the public space of appearance, moving it further towards the iconoclastic metaphysics of essences and appearances. That is the metaphysical mis-lead of the industrial beast. Its ultimate telos is the abyss, from which there is no possible recovery.

The industrial machinery of privatization is the logic of destruction at work in the public space; it subsumes everything to the production of end–points. Economics is the science of this subsumption, and it strives to realize its own end-point—a hierarchical human realm wherein only the privileged can appear to each other in all their splendor. The idealism of industrialism aims at this perfect, finally immutable, human type as its ultimate product. The telos of industrialism is the production of a being that cannot appear to others as other. Whether in the form of Hegel's absolute consciousness or Marx's victorious proletariat, or Adam Smith's enlightened self-interest seeker, this perfected type is kept concealed from the rebels de-constructing the texts of the regressive transformations of the public space. Industrialism proceeds by the delusion that it is itself capable of eradicating all traces of the Other. The eroscopher must dissemble this delusion if appearances are to be restored within a rejuvenated public space.

crinkum-crankum

The Other cannot appear within the composed industrial sensibility and its historical adjustment to the world of surfaces. "Adjustment" reads "author" rather than "Other"; it reads "cause" rather than "command." The effect of the industrially materialized symbol is a function of causal chains in which nothing is either added to or subtracted from their regulation of symbols.

The disappearance of the author and the apparition of the Other is simultaneously the de–composition of industrialized sensibility by the disrupture of surfaces become industrialized symbols. This is the preparation for the onset of creativity.

But the de–composition of industrialized sensibility, which attends the disrupture of the industrialized anti–world, also prepares the onset of madness—creativity without measure or the guidance of command.

Only afterwards does command supersede the unbounded nihilism of madness; it commands the retrieval of what has fallen through the cracks of the surfaces into the causal chains of industrialized production. Through and with the Other, this retrieval moves the impoverished economy of the industrialized anti–world into the superabundance of the just world.

Barjamming

being a nazi

It did not happen on the surface. In the abyss I became the Nazi that was within my subjected, coded body. This inscribed Nazi appeared with the spectacle of the ugly, the transformation of the public space. But the power of the ugly was no longer repulsive. On the contrary, becoming a Nazi was radiating within the wonderful privacy of its mis-lead. I did not turn away from the horror of the beast. I became instead the power of the horror, and it elevated me beyond equality. I became something with a transcendental warrant, an idealist that did not balk at what had to be done.

What must be done?

The future is burning, but it is only the future of weakness that is annihilated in my indifference. I have become the power that horrifies the weak ones I left behind. I relish this heightened perception. I do not yet know the source of the power that surges in my being, but I do know that it is the power that conquers death. Transfigured, I understand the symbolism of God on the cross. There is work to be done—all Jews must be turned to ash. I am the master of the Jew. It is my task to bring them to an end once and for all. I, a Nazi, experience completion in the exercise of my new being's power.

Remembrance? What turns to stone can never image. This is my spiritual task: the world must become one, true graven image: the cross as foreground, viciously crossing out all traces of the Other.

Not only must I remain decent through it all; I must come to feel decency as the necessary annihilation of everything and everyone limited by words, texts, imagings, thoughts. The burning children have brought me to my true self. What I must conquer is what I was before this glorious moment. To be born again, one must murder, without remorse, whomever and whatever holds one back. The new man does not hesitate, reflect, remember. Christianity was only the beginning. It is my task to complete what it started and then kill it too. One can remember only if one is different from that which one remembers. The One does not remember. My agony is that of the traces. They must be eradicated. How long can I be my true self if traces remain?

Occasionally, the cross recedes into the background. In my dreams—yes, I still dream—the bars of the cross fail to keep the background mute. I am sure it was an foul odor that woke me last night. It was vaguely familiar, although there is nothing like it in my new neighborhood. Perhaps, it was the new pipe tobacco I smoked before retiring. More likely, it was that strange cooking odor that came from my new neighbors next door. One must be vigilant: I will check them out.

I cannot help myself! I still feel that people are different in a threatening way. Two days ago I saw someone who brought some memories of things truly fantastic. Even though I know that such things are imaginary, I have begun to feel that even these imaginary things might be pointing to something real. But, even so, I do know that these possible realities are beyond me, the true self. Still, I am troubled because not everything reflects me, the one become true. My indifference has been disturbed.

But the Childrens' Park is a sacred place where indifference is always restored. No one knows the secret of its healing powers. I come here often to walk confidently on the seamless surface of this holiest of holies. There is no need to know when one feels its saving graces. Today, as I was leaving the park, I stumbled. The awareness of the trance came to me like a reference from the past. There was a tattered little note beckoning me from the stone next to my hand. I reached for it, this little thing that shattered my indifference, and awoke in a sweat.

There is something about being human that demands/demons. The demons told me the Park was overfilled with paria. It was as if a new word was being formed in me. I became a paranomasiac. It was impossible to keep quiet about this, words kept erupting through the cracks of my dementia. Silently they same, every night, and even daylight couldn't defend against them. Everything seemed different as the demonic words became the foreground of the old ones. I went to the Park and saw its surfaces weep.

Very carefully, I explained all of this to the Ariya. I was given a black stone with nine symbols engraven in gold. The array was fascinating. On each pulsation of the Unitary, I was ordered to trace the array with my index finger, beginning in the center, then once out to each of the other eight symbols. This crossing was to become compulsive, my second nature against the demons. I did this for six days and slept without demands for five nights. On the seven day, I awoke knowing that the Unitary was divided by nine. I began to anticipate the pulsations of the Unitary. Perversely, I began to vary the rhythms of my compulsive crossing. On the eighth day of my correction, I found my true self dancing with another. The demons were no longer inside me. I was steeped in the tears of the surface, bent to the stones which shatter indifference.

I felt the terrible pulse of the Ravensbrück memorial in Amsterdam. It was October 27, 1988. I was 300 meters away from Van Gogh's paintings. I decided to take a picture of the memorial. A woman stopped and addressed me in Dutch. I tried my Dutch, but then, in American, confessed my limits. In English, she asked whether I was taking a picture of the memorial because it was an interesting subject or because I believed in it. When I said "both," she proceeded to tell me her story. There are commandments which can only be heard in the vulnerability of the shattered self. After some moments of silence, she told me that she was a Jehovah Witness. I felt my Nazi self stir when she asked me if I believed that God would heal the earth. Hesitantly, I said "That's hard to believe." Moments of silence. She left asking if I would think about it. Is it possible that this old woman had not yet heard the news!

I took two more shots of the memorial.

I have never printed these negatives.

The Other, both *en dehors* and *de dedans*, is the mystery at the very heart of creativity. The abhorrence of *l'impureté* is the self–hatred of the *Schlecht-gekommenen*. In this the savage and technocrat are alike. The one sprays his habitat to neuter it, while the other neuters himself to spare his habitat. But we **are** the earth. The mystery is a living one.

Self-consciousness may well be the effect of a disease that feeds off whatever is healthy. Other than this self, always conscious of but never in control of itself, is that which gives. It gives even to the disease that grows against the gift. This Other is not given in the representations of self-consciousness, which represents only what it can appropriate. Representations present the appropriated Other, that is, the other as mine. Self-consciousness is projected narcissism.

Thus, it is not possible to reflect on disease in a non-diseased way. But, is it possible to see the disease as such? Could writing be a praxis that escapes the representations of self-consciousness? A terrifying question for philosophers. Are the latest metaphysicians the critics that punish all writing that responds to the traces?

There is one and there is Other: one another. With one another we are the response to the Other. *Antonumia*: a word used instead of another. *Autonomia*: a word used to deny the Other. Autonomy, sovereignty, but yet *sin, sinn, synthesis*, and even *send*. The eruption of the dialogue in even the most tightly constructed monologues: the demons of dementia—*Sinecure*.

The history of private property shows that a public place cannot be occupied. History is itself one of the public places which many professionals try to occupy. Thus, one simply can't have sex in public. Gender and gendering, especially gendarmary, take place elsewhere. Whatever shows something alienates it from its occupation. One can appear in public, but never in privacy. A recent newspaper headline tells us "The hostages enjoy their privacy." This shows why newspapers rarely show us anything.

Self-consciousness is obviously private, occupied. What is it then that makes us take leave of ourselves? If only we could have a self–directed life. Perhaps, this intense desire for sovereignty is the reason why actors are always associated with immorality. But acting and self–consciousness are antagonists. Yet, actors write autobiographies. Do their plays, films, and scripts deconstruct their autobiographies?

Is there a way of breaking codes that is not oppositional? Or, is everything and everyone binary? The demons mix–up the codes. Convolutions begin to replace the endless and repetitive pairings of the machine.

I no longer had even the slightest control over what popped–up. Pop–ulating does not op–pose cop–ulating, yet it is necessary to hyphenate to assure the gathering. Perhaps, Pop opposes Cop, people versus order. Versus: to turn is always to return: convolution—eternal return: a tautology: discipline of learning. The oppositions do not stay fixed; they . . . image.

We walked the way from the Viktualien Markt to the Deutsches Museum. On the way from living things to things of the past, I thought they might be the same since both were consumed these days. We are what we eat, no doubt. As the words began to play, I stood at the entrance of the Deutsches Museum. Something was not right or, rather, something was not present. I like museums because in these wonderful places, everything is always in its right time and place, everything so *museal*. But the words were still playing. As we entered the museum, I thought mausoleum. This time grabbed me: Grabmal—the German word seized me as we walked through the entrance. Imagings were everywhere. The *museal* images weren't in their proper places. Yet, no one else was seeing this horrifying transgression of the museum. I was just a visitor, and my spoken German wasn't that good either. I didn't even say anything about this onslaught of imagings to Suzette, who wanted very much to see the Chinese kite. Why was this happening to the Deutsches Museum, one of the many wonderful places which preserve a little from the stinking slicks of consuming flesh who flows of shit foul everything?

    We ate lunch.
    More word play.
    The next day, Dachau.

I showed the Dachau slides to my "Auschwitz and After" students. They asked questions of a factual nature. No problem. I thought of the Deutsches Museum and its imagings. Or, was it just my crazy imagination? I didn't tell my students about the imagings—such things are marginal notes, at best, in Academe, which, like the museum/mausoleum, has everything in the right order. How could I explain to my philosophy colleagues that I had to write a paper on images imaging? How could I justify taking so much time on such a marginal issue? Why was my Nazi self troubled by such things? Everything had been restored. The past was past and, as such, safely repressed.

Perhaps only Nietzsche understood that the realist who deals only with settled matters is the most repressed of all beings. How does one teach about the stones that teach differing together with the tears of the surfaces? A horrible thought occurred to me. It is the Nazi self that allows me to hear the stones!

My students feel very bad about what happened, but they do not feel implicated. They are not aware of the Nazi self that lives in us. Should I help them get in touch with their Nazi self? *Erfahrung,* but not *Erlebnis.* The words keep playing. This commanding of the Other is a very difficult journey.

"dummes Kind!"

Dachau
town and country

It was our second visit to Dachau. The weather was typically Münchenlike for early June. The rain had just ended as we pulled up to Hotel Burgmeier. On our first visit in 1986 we hadn't taken the time to see the town of Dachau, only the concentration camp on the outskirts. For the next four days we would see both Dachaus, always together despite the disarming charm of the town itself. Yes, always together. All towns and cities are like Dachau. Each and every one attempts to deny the conjunction which links them to the concentrationary universe in which we live. These denials are predominantly visual. As negations they are simple and easy images, but they become complex and uneasy images as they combine with the images of the Lager.

Neue Föhnstimmung in Dachau

Hofgarten

Friedhofskapelle

Alter Friedhof

Die Herrschaft der Sieben

Weiberlist

"du bist ein Mann, wenn . . ."

Unterwegs

Weg zum Kloster/Lager

Studie

Errinnerung an Dich

Das Ministerium

über die Stränge

Andenken

du kannst dir das nicht denken

Das Technikum

יד ומצבה
לזכר
רבבות הקדושים בני עמנו
אחינו ואחיותנו התמימים והטהורים
שנספו במקום ההריגה הזה
בשנות ת׳צ׳נ - תש׳ה
על ידי הרוצחים הנאצים
הוקם ביוזמתו של
איגוד קהילות בווריה
ת׳נצב׳ה
תשכ׳ז

Die Opfergabe

"da es nun einmal so ist"

Grab Tausender Unbekannter

Italienische KZ—Gedächtniskapelle

ein (Kloster) binden

Merkpunkt

Spiegelbild mit einem Spleiß

As the privatized and mythical idols of the regressive mislead are brought back to public disclosure, they antagonize the desire nurtured by that mislead and its promises. We do not want to see Dachau this way, this picturing of history in reverse and imaging of the goal of unbound transcendence. But is it really easier to go with the mis-lead despite what has happened? Or have our public spaces been so transmogrified that the shining appearances they alone make possible become instead terrible images of profoundly anti-political forces?

If Paul Celan could not give up on German and poetry after Auschwitz, knowing full well that neither could ever again be what they were before the devastation, should we give up on public disclosures knowing that they also can never be what they were before the terrible industry machines of privatization transformed them? To give up on language, art, and politics would concede the final victory to Hitler and his machines. But neither can we write, read, draw, and speak as if our mediums of freedom have remained untouched by what has happened.

After Auschwitz, easy images are one and all seductive misleads. The apparent transparency of photographs is especially seductive. Those powers in the service of the annihilating abyss prefer noiseless transmissions-transportations. Indifference is the *Stimmung* of invisible, noiseless techniques. In the sway of indifference our thinking becomes increasingly abstract and complicitous with the production of re-productive techniques that conceal their methods of transmission.

This series of photographs of the town of Dachau and the Dachau concentration camp, as well as all the other photographs in this book, have been reproduced in such a way that their material opacity and syntax remains just barely noticeable. Unfortunately, this manner of "noiseless" transmission tends to let us forget that the transcendence of art is both made possible and limited by the materials it shapes and is shaped by. Nazi idealism and the indifference which made possible its executions of "noiseless" transportations must be countered by an anti-aesthetic of representational surfaces—one which understands that after Auschwitz, every representational medium bears traces of that Event.

Thus, just as the town of Dachau is inseparable from its concentration camp, our representations of that uneasy image is itself implicated in what it attempts to critique. There is no unbound transcendence. Nor are there any cities without the uneasy images of Dachau.

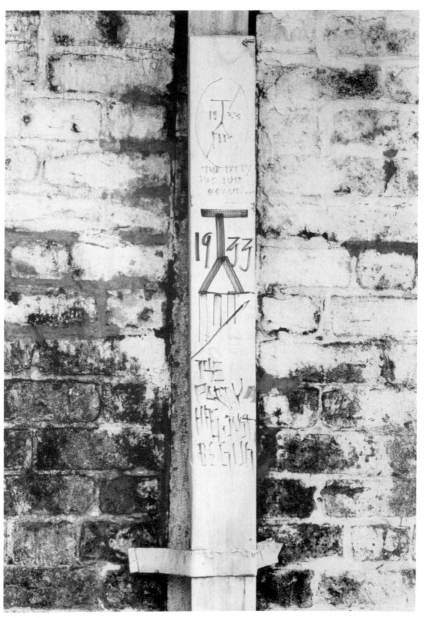

"The Party has just begun"

facet 4
joy and sorrow

The greatest joys pulling at our deepest sorrows?
Tears of happiness—our release to the outside?

No, it's not a metaphysical matter.

The historically specific configuration called beauty, the interplay of surfaces in the composing and decomposing of sensibility, is today only a trace
in the aftermath of State crimes which have fractured our sensibility. State
crime cracks the beautiful world in a radical way: the connection of touching
and thinking is broken, and thus the deformation of the world cannot be
retouched. The cracks of state crime lead into an abyss, a rupture that
separates us from what was and what is yet to come. If we were only what had
been written about us, we would never be able to overcome this separation.
Nor would we be able to enter this separation and survive if we were only
what we once were. But we have mutated and this is why the Nazis may not
have the last word.

Whenever a gap is exposed, everything in the order of economic interest
avoids this exposure. Our world is a multidimensional world, a world
become two and apart. The monological ego of one world is no longer ours,
which is why we have become eroscophers rather than metaphysicians. All
first principles, all authors, belong to the one–dimensional occlusion of what
the abyss discloses. The metaphysical mis-lead of economics works by re-
pressing the abyss it leads into. It is that specific repression which sustains
priority and authorship after Auschwitz.
The way into the occluded disclosure is a convoluted inscription of the
flesh, inside and out. But engraved bodies battle against this convoluted
inscription, insisting that every note of this inscription be played instead in
the registers of surfaces. The endless work of the Historians: to rewrite the
story of the ego's interruptions, irruptions, and demise so that synchrony
and diachrony are one, dialectically or otherwise. The wonderful effect of

this Re–visionary work is that in History logical connectives have no referents in the re–written, materialized world of first principles.

Still, the convoluted inscription of the flesh is also on the surfaces—the stones weep, and the compositions decompose. With the decomposing tears, ego differentiations are unglued. Moments of interruption, moments of mutated beings open to the outside, inside, and between, open to the multidimensional world of polyphonic possibilities other than those of ego interests.

But the cries of agony are too much! Back to business as usual! Back to the indifference of interests! Priority has always demanded sacrifices—there are limits to what the ego can accommodate. But, somehow, the mutants know it is more terrible to avoid the abyss and return to normalcy.

I promised not to forget. Yes, but I kept remembering this promise. There were inscriptions that made me remember my promise. When I first promised, I didn't know there were inscriptions that could undo one's very "being," everything that had been written about my type. When I promised to remember, I didn't understand that such a promise meant I could no longer sustain my transcendental identity.

Surfaces are barriers, interruptions of the exterior flows. Points, lines, planes of gatherings, folding inward–outward. I knew I was moving in these endless folds. I thought of Ariya and the black stone with its fascinating array. Then my body exploded, my ego receding into the manifold folds. All of us began our way back to the surface, where we emerged as tears in the concrete crevices of the walkway.

Convoluted thought is not dialectical; it knows of connections, but nothing of progress. Imaging is different from the imagination of the body–ego and its defenses against interruptions. Progress is an effect of ideology and meaning, an imaginary barrier constraining the eternal return.

    What returns?

    Imaging.

But the belief in progress is not inscribed, nor is it written over the scars of our touching bodies. To see the surfaces as healings and healed is to see the history of the broken bodies, synchrony punctuated by diachronies. To see this is to confront the guiltless as the level of guilt, which is the level of awareness and self–consciousness peculiar to the individual self. Being a Nazi is not yet the end of me!

Differentiations beginning with explosions inevitably become defensive barriers over and above one another, when writing, speaking, thinking, and making become systems of violence. Then follows the belief in progress and the illusion of priorities. What does not fit falls between the cracks. Priority occludes the cracks, the suffering of separation. Guilt, rupture, authorship: hard and fast words to drown–out the falling cries.

Beneath and above the economy of selves and their goals . . . that which cannot be represented, except by representations that undo themselves as they work. It is this subversive, fluid representation that enables idolatrous representation—the naming gives names without being named. This is what disturbs the illusion of constancy, the *vita contemplativa:* the exploding body, the very experience of being alive "in" two worlds. All around, somethings/ ones very cranky about disturbances of identity.

Yes, we live by the grace of sacrifice. Economies are very important systems of maintenance: one thing for another at a rate abstractly determined: economic representations and the formalism of art come together to say nothing beyond what they have been told to say.

Nothing moves anywhere without becoming bent. I remember my promise. I need to trace these representations. This is not the path of representations to other representations, but an oblique journey. Why? Because there is that unavoidable point at which words fall–off, where the chain of signification has been broken . . . but not yet severed! I need to find this point, this intersection where being a Nazi is interrupted by something cranky. I need crinkum–crankum! and the eternal circle of becoming: imaging against the idols, like Ariya and his black stones. I need to be with the non–represented representing, in love beyond the confines of the world's representational knowing. I want to be the ungraven power I have become. I want to stop the flow, appropriate its power.

Economies move on the basis of needs. Life moves in the flows of . . . . It is economy that speaks in my needs. For years I tried to become the things supplied by the economies. But surrounded with commodities, I could not become even one of them. I wanted Baudrillard's cynicism and his hyperreality, but there was always that agonizing difference. I tried to be a professional. I had professional things, did professional things, and professed many things. I wrote like a professional, but still could not become One. I was moderately successful, but could not become that modicum of success. These essences were different from me, or rather, I was always differing from them. I also tried to become a good, respectable, and caring person, but these essences also differed. I didn't fit anything, anywhere, anytime. Yet, I joined organizations like other well–intentioned people. Lacking neither intent nor talent, I could not be any of the things offered by the economies. Each time I tried, there was that point at which . . . .

Perhaps, a different economy, I thought. I became a socialist, but that essence escaped me the same way that the Middle Ages failed to realize its Concept. Dialectics is a powerful weapon for the *Schlechtgekommenen,* but its sleight of hand is always too visible for mutants: dialectic is the way representations keep their falling–off points unnoticed. Why, then, couldn't "I" trip this light fantastic? I kept thinking of Ariya. Where was my black stone? Promising to remember incapacitates pre-mutant memory.

Perhaps, a system of true justice? A beautiful array of distributions. Where was my black stone? A faint glimmer of my old self.

Perhaps, a faith? Did I really need my black stone?

Perhaps.

Problems, nothing but problems. Was this the eternal becoming, problems which refused to stay solved? But there must be final solutions! I had learned my Plato: to establish something better, one had to know the Good. Plato said that, and it made sense only as long as you didn't heed the many falling–off points of "his" texts. There is another reading: you can never **appropriate** anything, especially yourself.

I began to hear Socrates and Ariya in dialogue. Socrates, the great un–doer, different from the one the "followers" of Plato engraved in stone. The "great ones"—those who have followers. I thought of Zarathustra and his followers. This is what I wanted to be: a great teacher whose words were repeated, "quoted." To establish a body of knowledge! A chain of significations without interruptions! But then I remembered. I had promised not to forget. Forget what?

I was certain, however, that things weren't arbitrary. If there were no final solutions, a nagging nihilistic possibility, there were economies. Presence was certain! Even if everything solid melted, there was something melting. The Greeks had it right: there must **be** something that becomes. Without this, no knowledge, no bodies, no egos, no feeling of certainty, no way to live amidst the chaos. The imperative was clear. Everything that had been hammered–out must be preserved and safe–guarded. Without the tradition, we are nothing! But it was the plurality of tradition that was troublesome. Everything tried and true, but in contention with itself. The final solution.

trauming

Why does everything have to be coherent, rational, exchangeable only as equivalences? The chaos which I am as a continuous part of the dual world universe does not raise this question. It is the discontinuous, separated being **I am**, the interior, which battles the chaos I am, that **demands** its place in the sun. Nietzsche, that tormented devil, said "It thinks, rather than I think." But Freud, a great concealing unconcealer, turned Nietzsche on "his" It: "I think because It desires too much." Thinking is the maker of compromises, or needs, which, in time, become more or less rational. Or, does our thinking becomes more and more demanding? **There will be truth!**

It is me when I am not alive: I am it when it is power: power and life no longer opposites, but . . . . I cannot be alive and be continuous, except for those lapses: the living dead. Why am I most full of myself when separated from everything else? Most alive when most full of myself?

I "had" a dream. Upon awakening, a calm insight. Theater and the dream are the same, except the theater has been taken over by philosophers. In "my" dream the stage remained the same throughout a series of acts, in each of which the characters changed as the story unfolded. I desired the woman in Act 1, but she was transformed into a man in Act 3. The man in Act 1 was seduced by the woman in Act 2. I resented the man of Act 1 and desired the one of Act 2, at least I think this was the sequence of the story. The woman of Act 1 was close to me, but the woman of Act 3 was from my distant past. Why was I so calm upon awakening? My discontinuous self should have recoiled from these continuous "identities." "Who" came upon the insight? Can one see into anything/one and remain the same? Does the chaotic exterior become the interior chaos repeated traumatically? Folded over, I returned to sleep.

We sleep when things make sense. We dream because the sense of things is a creation of personal desire. Even the philosophers understand this! There is something obscene next to every meaning? Or, perhaps, the obscene is the theater of meaning–acts? Words–characters: exchangeables coupling according to certain rhythms. Nietzsche again: music is the mother of language. Mother? M[(u{s)(ic})]other: Mere formulaic musing, no doubt. But then, some words are **called**: Names, especially the proper ones. Discontinuity is duplicated in language, which is no system other than the open one that makes discontinuities. Here one could repeat a discourse on language. But why? The same refrain each repetition: if you play/sleep with one, you play/sleep with all—the "all" being the fiction that lures all into the never ending story. To give meaning to the chaos is to duplicate the chaos from the inside. The more one writes, the crazier one becomes. This dream was not calming. I heard the **call** that brings "reality."

my calling

I heard, but hesitated. A voice can freeze, as can a vision, touch, even an odor. One senses things and people, but only if not indifferent to discontinuity. The senses are reciprocal: one cannot touch anything and remain unchanged. For a moment, only an instant, one is continuous, gathered, with something/one else. Bataille writes beautifully of this instant. I noted that one can be coupled with someone else and still be discontinuous. Continuity, in the other world, is of the instantaneous order. Eternity is within the instant of that world apart.

After the rupture of continuity, one can only be a response. Other than the instant, there is only the order of the symbolic, the interior achievement of unity. How foolish to think that the symbolic has anything to do with what is called "representation." On this foolishness, Plato wrote beautifully. It is understandable, however, why his epigynies misunderstand him. They think that *one* can possess and be continuous after the rupture. I thought of Heidegger's appropriation of Being.

My calling? I have had several, each impossible and necessary. In flight from each, I became a number of things which others rightly took as representations of me. These are the representing ones I never touched. There have been a few, however, who . . . .

To live life as a perpetually delayed orgasm, to stay touching.

I heard the voices of the children, the future. I did not hesitate. The whole symbolic order came apart. To those who "knew" me—had representations large and small—I remained the same.

Concepts, relations, ideas, theories and ideologies come and go. I was no exception. For me, each and all of these departed, and then something marvelous happened. What profound joy! Their agony cut to the quick of my "being." The stones cried, my flesh convulsed, intellect disintegrated. Only for an instant, though . . . memories of what/who had been before this instant came to me.

I was touched, began anew, and became pro–missive.

When called, one responds after becoming a new discontinuity. We remember what we were because we are different from that which we remember. This is how discontinuity is gathered by an order it cannot appropriate. Without memory, there is no symbolism, no meaning. I promised not to forget, but as I write, I fragment memory. I thought of the woman in Act 2. We touched, and remembered as the thunder drew nearer.

The Failure of Self-Knowledge

intromission

Everything touches. Everything opens itself to violation. Everything violates what is other than itself, including itself. Humans, however, have sublimated a great deal of this violence. Only humans, perhaps, are on the long road to the perpetually delayed orgasm. Not really a road, long or short, but rather a labyrinth where the axe cuts a n–dimensional wound. The multi–selved self is such a wound. We come upon ourselves when we remember. Memory, however, is discursive. To write or tell a story that unfolds in one or two dimensions is to try and make one's audience forget themselves. Has the bourgeois novel rendered Homer incomprehensible? Did Freud parse Sophocles? Can I write today and keep my promise to remember?

To remember: to bear witness. Thus, writing as martyr, mindful of the suffering of touching the ones selected for spiritualized violence. Words— memoranda. To write after touching is to grieve in public. But I know what the economies will do with this.

notes for facets

Perhaps no writer since Plato has improved on the irony of moving away from appearances by means of appearances. To be sure, there are many who parted company with irony with a certain kind of absent-mindedness, a cultivated inattentiveness to the word as such. Our "tradition" comes from the latter; it teaches, but not without contradictory effects, that the more knowledgeable, the more competent and masterful one becomes, one's material is conquered and vanishes in the transparency of one's works—which require of course a certain kind of reader-student. And, as Plato warned in many ways, this tradition is "essentially" monological. Above all, it doesn't like to play and hates being played whenever it gets caught at work.

Heidegger, for one, has played with this tradition, without irony, but not I hope without contradictory effects. With a mastery the inattentive ones would be proud of, Heidegger, after many arduous and preliminary sketches, painted a very persuasive picture of contemporary society as modern subjectivity made absolute. It is, however, the framework of this picture that shows the hand that knowingly painted it—the hand that first wrote about depth—authenticity—resolve. Yet are there not always two hands, one that gives and another that erases—two hands at odds with one another? Do the two hands that hold the frame together in admiring appreciation forget the battles that kept them working?

Could deep cultivation, the reign of one dominant hand, the entire civilizing process, *Bildung*, be a preparation for cruelty? Is there a cultivation so deep that it prevents the soil from recovering?

"He has control of the other's scream of pain and death; he is master over flesh and spirit, life and death. In this way, torture becomes the total inversion of the social world, in which we can live only if we grant our fellow man life, ease his suffering, bridle the desire of our ego to expand. But in the world of torture man exists only by ruining the other person who stands before him. A slight pressure by the tool-wielding hand is enough to turn the other—along with his head, in which are perhaps stored Kant and Hegel, and all nine symphonies, and the World as Will and Representation—into a shrilly squealing piglet at slaughter. When it has happened and the torturer has expanded into the body of his fellow man and extinguished what was his spirit, he himself can then smoke a cigarette or sit down to breakfast or, if he has the desire, have a look in at the World as Will and Representation." [Jean Améry, *At the Mind's Limits: Contemplations By a Survivor On Auschwitz and Its Realities*, trans. Sidney Rosenfeld and Stella P. Rosenfeld (New York: Schocken Books, 1986), p. 35]

"Death is a possibility-of-Being which Dasein itself has to take over in every case. With death, Dasein stands before itself in its ownmost potentiality-for-Being. This is a possibility in which the issue is nothing less than Dasein's Being-in-the-world. Its death is the possibility of no-longer being-able-to-be-there. If Dasein stands before itself as this possibility, stands before itself in this way, all its relations to any other Dasein have been undone. This ownmost non-relational possibility is at the same time the uttermost one." [Martin Heidegger, *Being and Time*, trans. John Macquarrie and Edward Robinson (New York: Harper & Row, 1962), p. 294]

"Only if the inquiry of philosophical research is itself seized upon in an existentiell manner as a possibility of the Being of each existing Dasein, does it become at all possible to disclose the existentially of existence and to undertake an adequately founded ontological problematic." [*Being and Time*, p. 34]

"Dasein is authentically itself only to the extent that, *as* concernful Being-alongside and solicitous Being-with, it projects itself upon its ownmost potentially-for-Being rather than upon the possibility of the they-self. The entity which anticipates its non-relational possibility, is thus forced by that very anticipation into the possibility of taking over from itself its ownmost Being, and doing so of its own accord." [*Being and Time*, p. 308]

"All its relations to any other Dasein have been undone,"—this is what Améry experienced. Could the project of fundamental ontology be "seized upon in an existentiell manner as a possibility of the Being" of Jean Améry? Would it look any different than the fundamental ontology of those Daseins which served as the basis of *Sein und Zeit*? When Améry anticipated his non-relational possibility ("the total inversion of the social world," or what Heidegger prefers to call "das Man"), does he take over from himself, and of his own accord, his ownmost Being?

Well, Heidegger didn't read Jean Améry and he refused to discuss such "weighty" matters with Paul Celan. But Améry's answer is clear enough: "Whoever has succumbed to torture can no longer feel at home in the world." (*At the Mind's Limits*, p. 40) Is this what Heidegger had in mind when he talked about "the unearthly power to break us of the habit of abiding in what is essential"?

A provisional thesis: to avoid the metaphysical mislead into the abyss of cultivation, for it is indeed bottomless, we will rebel against the masters and remain semi-literate (semiterate) in the memory of the many who knew so much more, wrote so much better, had all nine symphonies as part of their spirit, but returned to a world where the word was lost. Whereas Heidegger took ruination as an occasion for a profound transformation of Stefan George's verse "Kein ding sei wo das Wort gebricht" into "Ein 'ist' ergibt sich wo das Wort zerbricht" ["Das Wesen der Sprache," *Unterwegs zur Sprache* (Tübingen: Neske, 1971), p. 216], we will try to keep what remains from the whirlwind of the abyss.

Eroscophy is not for the profound ones whose cultivated desire is satisfied only in and by the simulations of mastery. It is not against the profound, but always suspicious of its finalities: "'Profundity has never clarified the world, Clarity looks more profoundly into its depths,' Arthur Schnitzler once said. Nowhere was it easier than in the camp, and particularly in Auschwitz, to assimilate this clever thought." [*At the Mind's Limits*, p. 20]

The eroscophical meanderings of the semiterate always rebel against any threat to the fragile solidarity of what remains of the social world. We must resist the pull of the great monologue of Being, especially when that monologue holds out the promise of an authentic and solicitous Being-with on the basis of non-relational possibilities.

If the inquiry of philosophical research can be seized "in an existentiell manner as a possibility of the Being of each existing Dasein," then it can be thus seized as a possibility of those who have been ruined in and by the world of torture. Surely there is no other site more conducive to the anticipation of Dasein's non-relational possibility than that of torture. And yet, Améry tells us that no one ever really recovers from torture.

No, you say, Heidegger wasn't thinking of that site. Fair enough, but then we must ask: What specific sites was he thinking of? Or, more urgently, which site was he speaking from? These are questions refused by Heidegger, who always withdrew into a conserving self-concealment when facing inquiries concerning the "existentiell" loci of his thinking. He steadfastly rejected suggestions that biographic information might make his thinking more accessible and thus intelligible to the uninitiated. The "essential" has nothing to do with such "superficiality."

Heidegger's powerful critique of modern subjectivity, one from which I draw in the sections "the hell of subjectivity" and "the fine style," is not, however, a self-critique. Heidegger did not reveal himself as implicated in what he critiqued. Instead he sought an "adequately founded ontological problematic" without the existential ambiguity and struggle necessarily involved in that founding. And surely this has something to do with the "demands" of academic publication and philosophical "research." At the risk of sounding *ad hominem*: "Heidegger cultivated an entirely different style with his students than the other professors. We went on excursions together, hikes and ski trips. The relationship to national culture [*Volkstum*], to nature, and also to the youth movement were, of course, talked about then. The word *national* [*völkisch*] was very close to him. He did not connect it to any political party. His deep respect for the people [*Volk*] was also linked to certain academic prejudices, for example the absolute rejection of sociology and psychology as big-city and decadent ways of thinking." (Max Müller, "Martin Heidegger" in *Martin Heidegger and National Socialism*, p. 178) This link between one's respect for (the) people and certain academic prejudices is indeed deeply involved in the "founding" of his ontological problematic. Thus, the texts in *Between Auschwitz and Tradition* attempt a critique of that "founding" and its academic prejudices. But, again, it is important to understand one's complicity in what one is critiquing.

The question of the place from which one reflects, theorizes, and writes is also the question of bodies. A fragmented and engraved body that appeals to transcendental warrants to speak in the name of the One may be much more than naive; it is a dangerous body that seeks mastery and unification by the displacement of others from the scene. Movements and voices that do not fit within master narratives are erased, denied representation, or distorted within a totality that sacrifices diversity and complexity for the sake of an impoverished totality. No one denied representation can afford to take such discourse at face value.

In the case of patriarchy and its privileging of the male subject, some men are just beginning to realize that their privileged position is a disempowering one. The poverty of discourse that evades threats to its centering becomes evident in its ever-increasing abstractness, a characteristic that renders it less and less capable of the mastery it so desperately seeks. The power of discourse is inversely proportional to its displacements, exclusions, and denials. In different ways this has been brought to the surface in the works of Foucault and Derrida, to mention just two examples of privileged male subjects coming to terms with their privileges.

In a discourse that seeks affinity rather than identity and mastery, Donna Haraway writes: "It is no accident that the symbolic system of the family of man—and so the essence of woman—breaks up at the same moment that networks of connection among people on the planet are unprecedentedly multiple, pregnant, and complex. 'Advanced capitalism' is inadequate to convey the structure of this historical moment. In the Western sense, the end of man is at stake. It is no accident that woman disintegrates into women in our time." ["A Manifesto for Cyborgs," *Feminism/Postmodernism*, ed. Linda Nicholson (New York: Routledge, 1990), p. 202] The monologue of Being ends when Being can no longer speak to men in the voice called the Law of the Father. "Papa's Sermon" is no longer the call of conscience.

In the section called "the abyss" I say "The depths are really the surface." This follows a fictional/experiential account which moves from the surfaces to the depths or foundations of Western civilization. The revealed depths are now the surfaces of our existence, our "thrownness" if you will. The depths or foundations are the product of both our imaginary projections and an unsurpassed arrogance that replaced the finite and contingent subject with that special subject, the "I" that demands as its own command the principle of non-contradiction. Heidegger's analysis of the evolution of modern thought and its radical transformation of ancient thought is still unsurpassed. In the second volume of his Kant study, Heidegger describes what is "essential" in Descartes thinking: "Only where thinking thinks itself is it absolutely mathematical, i.e., a taking cognizance of that which we already have. Insofar as thinking and positing directs itself toward itself, it finds the following: *whatever* may be asserted, and in whatever sense, this asserting and thinking is always an 'I think.' Thinking *is* always an 'I think,' *ego cogito*. Therein lies: I am, *sum. Cogito, sum* —this is the highest certainty lying immediately in the proposition as such." [*What is a Thing?*, trans. W. B. Barton, Jr. and Vera Deutsch (Chicago: Henry Regnery, 1970), p. 104] For Heidegger, this is a radical change of Dasein, "of the illumination of the being of what is on the basis of the predominance of the *mathematical* " (p. 106).

But what casts suspicion on Heidegger's claim that subjectivism and its radical transformation of thought steers modernity into the dominance of science and technology is Nietzsche's observation that rather than "I think" we should say "It thinks." [*Jenseits von Gut und Böse* (Frankfurt am Main: Insel, 1984), p. 26] In other words, the radical transformation is a question of bodies and their respective positions. Freud was the first after Nietzsche to develop the critique of the self-posited rational (mathematical) foundations of modernity. Freud, however, is never mentioned by Heidegger. In his discussion of Newton and Galileo, Heidegger says: "Concerning the basic law of motion, the law of inertia, the question arises whether this law is not to be subordinated under a more general one, i.e., the law of the conservation of energy which is now determined in accordance with its *expenditure* and *consumption*, as *work*—a name for new basic representations which now enter into the study of nature and betray a notable accord with economics, with the 'calculation' of success." Is this a hint that oppressed bodies and their social positions have something to do with the founding of modern thought? No, because Heidegger follows these lines with: "All this develops within and according to the fundamental mathematical position" (p. 94). This is and always has been the line of defense against philosophy's contamination by the other(s).

This is not to say that what Heidegger says about modern thought is wrong. What he does not say about the beginnings of modern thought is, however, troubling. Nowhere does Heidegger even suggest that what he displaces under the rubric of the mathematical has something to do with the rebellion against Church authority and the socio-political systems which sustained that authority. This would be "inessential" or merely derivative in the Heideggerian framework. But here it is instructive to compare Heidegger's treatment of the transition from ancient to modern thought and metaphysics with John Dewey's treatment in *The Quest for Certainty* (1929) and his earlier formulations in *Reconstruction in Philosophy* (1920). Bearing in mind Heidegger's characterization of American philosophy (pragmatism) as identical (in essence) to Soviet communism, I would like to quote two passages from *Reconstruction in Philosophy* : ". . . inquiry is free only when the interest in knowing is so developed that thinking carries with it something worth while for itself, something having its own esthetic and moral interest. Just because knowing is not self-enclosed and final but is instrumental to reconstruction of situations, there is always danger that it will be subordinated to maintaining some preconceived purpose or prejudice. Then reflection ceases to be complete; it falls short. Being precommitted to arriving at some special result, it is not sincere. It is one thing to say that all knowing has an end beyond itself, and another thing, a thing of a contrary kind, to say that an act of knowing has a particular end which it is bound, in advance, to reach. Much less is it true that the instrumental nature of thinking means that it exists for the sake of attaining some private, one-sided advantage upon which one has set one's heart." "Anything that in a given situation is an end and good at all is of equal worth, rank and dignity with every other good of any other situation, and deserves the same intelligent attention." [*Reconstruction in Philosophy*, enlarged edition (Boston: The Beacon Press, 1957), pp. 145-46 and p. 176]

If, in other words, philosophy is and always has been "infected" by struggling bodies, historicity and contingency, that does not mean that philosophy as a self-positing master narrative has to be thrown out when such narratives become no longer credible. In a very intelligent and politically sensitive article, Nancy Fraser and Linda J. Nicholson critique Jean-François Lyotard's postmodern position: "He goes too quickly from the premise that Philosophy cannot ground social criticism to the conclusion that criticism itself must be local, ad hoc, and nontheoretical. As a result, he throws out the baby of large historical narrative with the bathwater of philosophical metanarrative and the baby of social-theoretical analysis of large-scale inequalities with the bathwater of reductive Marxism class theory. Moreover, these allegedly illegitimate babies do not in fact remain excluded. They return like the repressed within the very genres of postmodern social criticism with which Lyotard intends to replace them." ["Social Criticism without Philosophy," *Feminism/Postmodernism*, p. 25] Lyotard thus suffers from the same binarism (metaphysical oppositions) that he purports to reject on the basis of the postmodern condition. Craig Owens is right when he says "we have to learn how to think difference without opposition." ["The Discourse of Others: Feminists and Postmodernism," *The Anti-Aesthetic: Essays on Postmodern Culture*, ed. Hal Foster (Port Townsend: Bay Press, 1983), p. 62]

The return of the repressed, the master narratives of modernity, the commanding of the special subject "I think," can either be worked-through or reenacted. "Facet 3: the idealism of economic disclosure" is my attempt to work-through the texts which continue to write and speak us. We are implicated in these master narratives, but there are also displaced texts which our implicated bodies can bring to the surface. Bodies do not evolve without complicity, without that nodding approval so often sought by the masters who teach us in the authority of the commanding subjectum.

To let our bodies speak the way they have been written is to repress what we have become "in the light of" transformative events. It is to continue a tradition as if nothing happened to cast suspicion on that tradition and its remarking of our bodies. It does not want to come to terms with the fact that the Nazism was no aberration, that the Nazis were both revolutionaries and idealists [see Alfred Kazin, "The Heart of the World," *Auschwitz: Beginning of a New Era?*, ed. Eva Fleischner (New York: KTAV, 1977) and George M. Kren, "The Holocaust: Moral Theory and Immoral Acts," *Echoes from the Holocaust: Philosophical Reflections on a Dark Time*, eds. Alan Rosenberg and Gerald E. Myers (Philadelphia: Temple University Press, 1988)]. The photograph "Barjamming" is just one of many reminders that the return of the repressed is all too common today.

This is also the theme of "Dachau: Town and Country," but here transposed onto the register of visual images. Since I have written elsewhere about how images work for the state against us and how they can work with and for us when they are transformed into uneasy images ["Easy Becoming Uneasy Images: A Photogrammic Solarization of Caves," *Continental Philosophy, Vol. V: Questioning Foundations*, ed. Hugh J. Silverman (New York: Routledge, 1993)], I will not repeat myself here. The sequence and juxtapositions of the photographs do, I hope, move from easy to uneasy images of what we can no longer afford to repress or simply reiterate.

Facet 4 returns to the other of (modern) philosophy, the body no longer chained by the cogito and by its seductive authoritarian pull of authorship. The ego is undone by the destructions of the surface which interrupt and disturb its abstractions. We find ourselves with the devil in Doctor Faustus, who Lyotard identifies as Adorno: "He is determined not to make 'Auschwitz' into an episode. Thought remaining in the abyss, confronted with its own disaster, is struggling not to continue along its representational line but to approach what it has not been able to think and what it cannot think" (*Heidegger and "the jews,"* p. 43). Yet, the other world, the tradition, calls. Representations arise as respite. "I" am both identity and non-identity—"alive 'in' two worlds" that do not commune in the language of the cogito.

The remainder of "facet 4" is a provisional hetero-biographical "representation" of recovering representations haunted by that which cannot become an episode. It is close to what Derrida calls another economy. This other "economy would not be an energetics of pure, shapeless force. The differences examined *simultaneously* would be differences of site and differences of forces. If we appear to oppose one series to the other, it is because from within the classical system we wish to make apparent the noncritical privilege naively granted to the other series by a certain structuralism. Our discourse irreducibly belongs to the system of metaphysical oppositions. The break with this structure of belonging can be announced only through a *certain* organization, a certain *strategic* arrangement which, within the field of metaphysical opposition, uses the strengths of the field to turn its own stratagems against it, producing a force of dislocation that spreads itself throughout the entire system, fissuring it in every direction and thoroughly *delimiting* it." [Jacques Derrida, *Writing and Difference*, trans. Alan Bass (Chicago: The University of Chicago Press, 1978), pp. 19-20] This delimiting of metaphysical conceptuality is precisely one of site, of touching bodies remaining discontinuous for all of that. The task is to find "an inscription of the relations between the philosophical and the nonphilosophical, in a kind of unheard of *graphics*, within which philosophical conceptuality would be no more than a *function*" (*Writing and Difference*, pp. 110-111). The delimiting and unheard of graphics are respectively the themes of Part II and Part III.

PART TWO

The

W
E
A
K
E
N
####### I
######## N
######### G

representing becoming bent

wave 1
spilled innards

Subjects copulated and connected with other kinds. Then came the idea of predication and safe grammar: statements made by subjects about their proper associations. Much later, after the formations of the strong state, people began to express this appropriated tradition and its consummation: "get fucked!" As Marx would say, the world had become philosophical and philosophy would soon become worldly. And, indeed, today philosophers are very worldly as they write the world's "progress."

Despite its usage–meaning, however, getting "fucked," as Genet has pointed out, is to lose the one who "thought" he was doing the fucking. Thus, we come upon Sartre's w(hole)—Nothing. Had he been more unworldly and unHegelian, Sartre would have begun with Something rather than the Nothing of proper Being.

After the institutionalization of mass murder, we know what it means to get "fucked." So, we begin not with Being, nor with Nothing, nor with both, nor with Something, but rather with people and all their improper connections.

Adorno's memorandum

Upon reaching a stand–point, stand against it. To think is to think against what idolaters take as established and fixed.

To think: imaging against the appropriations of thought—bodies of knowledge. We are those things, bodies of knowledge, but we also think against what we are. Thinking is a movement of anti-bodies of knowledge. Which is why our "being" is other than appropriated traditions and their well-formed social selves. No matter how much the weight of inscriptions, we remain con–texts (contingent and fragile connections)—spoken and speaking anti-bodies against the graven images of appropriated thought. Touching transgresses tradition, not by destroying or repudiating it but by bringing it to life. Against the internal coherence which is the reward of societies ruled by death (idols), thinking in the abyss between the worlds, introduces itself as the other of safe grammatical associations.

rubric "ruby ruse"

Thinking remembers what is to come: rusty rubes of stainless artifices. What is to come? What was and is repressed by the terror of the dominant systems of reference. The future is suspended in the abyss, and repression concerns it. The codes of the orders undisturbed by the abyss are always split into leaves; their arbitrariness is a function of their inherent con–textuality. The various illusions of centeredness are one and all the Unitary of some ethnocentric hegemony. Is this a hi–story of power(s)? How could the absolutely centered, unitary, masculine subject be undone if it wasn't anything but the signified of arbitrary codes working for, besides, and against one another? Codes, especially when interleaved, undo themselves in their great silences.

But is this undoing the work of the arbitrary codes themselves? A question of punctuation! To emphasize, to centralize, is to interrupt the flow of signifiers. Thus, "things" come and go, in different times and spaces, and thus image the history of grammar and the violence which sustains it.

All the great word orders are derivations of various graven images. And each of these great orders has proven incapable of maintaining its graven "foundations."

Consider the gramophone, a device enabling the graven images to speak. The gramophone is a kind of transposing machine. Would this be possible if the codes were not arbitrary? Or, does the trans–posing obey the commands of an Urcode? Are there tablets so graven they command in the greatest silence? I cannot imagine such tablets as anything but split. All movement is a turbulence that up–sets. *Legein* is earlier than *graphein*. The bleeding stones undo all graven images. I want to bring these stones to all the grammar schools.

time's up

How many times must it be written?
　　As many as there are people,
　　　　　living, dead, yet to be.
　　Is there enough time?

　　Ground zero—ego time.
　　　　　　　　　　　But
duration—between me and you.
We're here for the duration.

　　　　Du, you, ration–ality.
　　　　　　Between us . . .
　　suspended
　　there is
　　no scarcity of time.

fixed time

　　When we see—
　　　imaging is no image.
One cannot see
　　　another seeing.
I see . . . after the seeing!

　　　When —
Seeing: the abundance between us
What we see: timeless,
　　　no height,
　　　alone, no us—
　　　image.

seeing

To be seeing —
      is not to see.
If you see,
      you are alone—
           ground zero.

Seeing—never a scene.
See—
      always timeless
      suspended
image play.

How many times must it be seen?
Too many possibles—
      an endless image play.
Seeing: du rationality.
Me, you . . . seeing together,
        no image are we.

Everything is a drawing,
      mark,
      inscription.
But not all is a thing,
Not all is written.

Silence does not hide,
      conceal,
      encode,
      protect.

Writings arrive,
      are sent,
         imagings—

Seeing.

Transmission cannot be seen.

The seen you see,
a meaning—scarcity of time,
fixed time,
images,
seeing fallen from du ration
Connecting, the images arrive.

the end of time looking backwards

phoslegs

All art resides in gathering, a folding–in that intensifies within the frame. Unlike the window that isolates and protects the viewer from the view, the frame of the gathering gathers the artist into the increase that often overwhelms.

Reading, writing, speaking are all responses to the frame which gathers. What cannot be read, written, or spoken is the gathering frame. The history of the frame is folded–in the gathering which increases and precedes its story. The various orders within the frame are preceded by the bringing–forth–of–order in the increase. It is the increase that disseminates the orders of other frames which have run their course of increasing. By the time we respond to the frame, the artist has already folded–in: artists are always untimely.

We can never respond *in kind* to that which calls us forth. Levinas has taught us that all philosophy is a response: we bear testimony as hostages never equal to the call, which increases with every response. With the increasing, responsibility beyond the confines of the individual ego that must bear it. The easy ways are the ways of turning–away from the increasing, overwhelmed by its power. The hard way is the response that keeps responding polyphonically.

The way of idolatry is the one that characterizes Western hi–story. I used to practiced it religiously and secularistically. The idols: frames read, written, and spoken *as such*. Idols cancel increasing responsibility; they place the gathered on the same footing as the gathering folding–in. Idolatry arrives whenever and wherever something/one finds a place under the sun. Idols are the selves which dominate and demand totality. Idols are all the voices of authority, often coming from gramophones.

Thus the various attempts at figuring–out things, as if the gathering were a ruse. It is the flight from responsibility that sustains representational projects. Short of irresponsibility, this flight is necessary for survival. A very hard lesson: total responsibility is also idolatrous.

It is not so unusual, then, that uneasy moderns represent our ship-wrecked age as "postmodern." Modernist theorists always speak in kind; they have the framing figured–out. The idol of modernism lifts the burden of responsibility with its idols of authorship—universality—the subject, as if the suspension were not there. In their postmodern mode, however, there are no hierarchical principles; it is one of an–archy, an inverting agitation of top and bottom, a helter–skeltering (collage) of previous orders and their great words.

For the easy modernists, on the other hand, all of this is not arbitrary; it is sustained by an intense morality, a bringing to bear of authoritative moral judgments against the postmodern attacks on authority. Modernism de-contextualizes the postmodern contextualization because the contingent, improper connections of the latter are, for them, the scandal that conveniently displaces the disaster separating the two worlds.

From the modernist perspective, the artists have done too good a job of revealing what has happened to previous orders. Modernism attempts to capture the postmodern condition, the mutation, within its universal grid, as if "we" were still free to arrange everything according to our social, alienated needs.

The modernist portrayal of postmodernism goes something like the following: postmodernism unleashes the dialectic of the grid at the level of the base, the common, the populace, against its capture by the elite; it is semiological Marxism played by the electric guitar at ear–splitting decibels; it is the art of the vulgar rocking the establishment that rolls along in the display and, like all idolatry, becomes desperate as the authorities purchase and display the contextualizations of authority. But for the postmodernist, any publicity (representing the represented, imaging the idols) is better than none in a modern unworld of almost pure privacy.

This self-portrayal is what drove Baudrillard to his modernist despair. All idolatry, especially that of the modernist, is not only self–destructive. It is also the stuff out of which repressions are made.

The artist belongs to the gathering in a way that is extraordinary. As the one who experiences the call to respond in the most intense way, she experiences the infinite gap, desire, between what is given and what is called–for. Nothing is ever good enough for the artist, who is bound in the service of the calling–forth. Hostage to this call, the artist can never have anything to do with things–done, except to un–do them, to liberate them from their completion (idolatry). Opposed to this incessant undoing activity of artists, we find the practitioners of the real, the hard–core men. They bring things to–an–end. At their end–points, things are lifeless and, as such, become disposable items. A real man has definition and defines others. The practical ones, including the moralists, square the circle much like Aristotle squared Heraclitus' flux.

Practicality resists framing as a folding–in(crease) of responsibility. The practical ones are the ones who think they possess the frame. They are the ones who do not hear, see, or feel the silent, invisible, and intangible calling–forth of folding–in. They have handled too many things and people at their end–points, the non–imaging. They are the ones who sponsor modernist productions. Despair is always a cash nexus.

But images image: "the stones weep" is poetic, but neither representational nor metaphorical. The imaging is what we call "seeing." Seeing touches what is invisible and incapable of being represented. What works against any comprehension of this is the metaphysical doctrine of things as substances and accidents. "Images imaging" does not mean the transcendental commerce of essences or the physiological collision of accidental matters. Seeing is not the same as looking–at–some–thing. All techniques of reproduction promote and depend upon looking–at. Images imaging, unlike reproductions, touch invisibly and sound silently; they are light and sound gathered in a silent intensification that moves to response.

A phosleg brings the past through the abyss which separates the worlds. It is a legacy that has come through, rather than around the abyss. The legacy of light today comes through the thick opacity of the disaster. Which is why art is no longer either "pretty" or realistic. Phoslegs do not deny what has happened, but neither do they "represent" the end of the world. There is art after Auschwitz, but it is neither fine art nor kitsch.

To–gathered, phoslegs are responses to all graven images. Phoslegs bring traditions to life, to us in the only way it is possible to have traditions after Auschwitz. Without passing through the abyss, traditions are dead, mere representations of history. Untransformed representations are impotent to move us because we have changed. We have mutated and become different than anything the appropriated traditions have written about being human. The universal grid of the modernists is a trap, a deadly device for figuring and capturing us. There is no simple or easy way of going from one world to another. And this is why we must deconstruct all the easy images by making them images within images—uneasy images. Everything, including modernism, must pass through the whirlwind which devoured the six million.

The abyss cannot be represented, and this is why modernism cannot help us in our task. Strictly speaking, there is no postmodernism, only the mutated postmodern condition. This is the mutated, postmodern response to the universal grid of the modernists. There is no other "place" for them or us. We are responses, and always suspicious of explanations, ideologies, theories, and especially of ethics. We cannot accept, even with qualifications, accounts of what we are and why we are. We are not things with a why or a mission but rather strange connective tissues, a new unnatural community that has emerged from the death camps mutilated but as yet undefeated. For us, there is no choice but to remember.

Phoslegs are "what" we are, and we bring strange new messages for those with old ears and eyes. Responses transform this "what" into who we are. We are the community of survivors bringing the old through the flames.

wave 2
assimilations

between points

Parabolic cones of light-matter intersect, forming configurations of re-flected and refracted energies. Some of these are the sensual images of consciousness. Looked at edgewise, the imaging self has a variable depth within these shifting intersections. Self–consciousness, an interruption of reflections and absorption of refractions, but always attempting to make these reflections its own, disappears with the dissolving of intersections. In nature there is no lasting unity of self-consciousness. Self-consciousness is a matter of contingent connections beyond the power of the appropriating ego. In the absence of connections, we are left with only memories, traces.

The unity of self-consciousness is multiple, marked by the hyphens of writing. The I of the self is the eyepiece that focuses the occasional interruptions of the cones of reflection. It is only because of the multi–elemented constitution of the eyepiece that the self can clearly and without distortion assimilate the cone's intersection. The self, however, is rarely mindful of its multiple constitution. Unity comes from multiplicity, but we remember multiplicity from the standpoint of achieved unity. Interruptions of our unity are reminders of its derivative status and, thus, occasions for achieving new ones.

The eye(I)piece does not see. The layer behind I, the absorbing one most active when I am interrupted, sees. Thus, seeing is a imaging feeling, a motion within a resisting medium that only lets go in that motion. There are many layers of feeling. It is the multidimensional seer that I do not see. I can come and go but never the seer which is never mine. Resistant identity is not found at the level of mineness.

Mere images? No doubt. But also a reminder that images, the ones our many precious egos would like to be done with, are still haunting us, reminding us that it is time for new selves.

Authenticity

selenic selves

I did not like what I saw in him. How could anyone have turned–out so poorly. Yet, there was something fascinating about the monster, his eerie presence, voice, and fanatical sense of mission. I felt this, but did not like what I saw. Of course, everyone sending me these images was saying that he was our hated enemy. But the cynical film industry didn't really understand that image and message are different things. I was then too young to grasp this propaganda war.

Every week, just about, a package or two would arrive. My uncle sent home wonderful toys: Nazi flags, Lugers, rifles (German and Japanese), spent shells of all sizes, helmets , uniforms, bayonets, insignias, decorative medals, and other assorted spoils of war. My friends seem to know when these packages had arrived and, soon, we were playing war with the real things. The Nazi flag with its captivating swastika was everyone's favorite. One morning I draped a huge one over the bushes in front of my grandparents' house. It was a real spectacle. I wasn't spanked for this, but my grandmother was unequivocal in her admonition. Above all, I remember her fear. I thought then that the flag episode was why she didn't allow me to take one of the many Lugers with me to see the latest weekly newsreel at the movies that Saturday. I liked the Lugers very much, they had a certain feel.

Kids live in a world of felt qualities. I remember that Sunday morning, different from the others. We always went to the early service, but this Sunday was different. The Pastor spoke in English. It was strange experience. I actually understood some of the service and hymns. Before this Sunday, the early service was in German. That had never mattered to me since I only attended to the tones, rhythms, shapes, colors, and especially to the strange smells coming from the women.

My grandfather never attended church. Later my father told me that he used to be Catholic but had given up on it. I lived with my grandparents during the two years my mother was in the hospital stricken with tuberculosis. I didn't see much of my father since he worked eighteen hours a day, six days a week. My grandmother was my guardian, teacher, and spiritual advisor. She was very unlike my grandfather who, when not working, instructed me in the arts of smoking White Owl cigars, drinking Pabst Blue Ribbon beer, and chewing Plowboy tobacco. I remember those smells well. He also tried to tutor me in the significance of listening to the police calls on the radio. But I only focussed on the static, which was always more frequent than the calls themselves.

I also remember the carpet on the floor with its wonderfully baroque design and distinctive smell. There was also that incredibly beautiful play of light that filtered through the lace curtains. Wonderful forms and textures, mixed with those warm, inviting smells. This was my earth separated from the outside world.

My private things were somehow different from the things in the world, a difference I did not understand. Yet, it moved me in different ways. The Nazi flag had a quality different than the things of my earth. The latter I sheltered from overexposure while the former seemed to demand display. When I draped it over the bushes, it was as if I was responding to its demand to be displayed. Later, I understood its captivating power: the rush of hate, call to duty and assault.

When I began to read books more complex and exciting than school textbooks, I discovered my sheltered things could be shared with others who also sheltered these things. Reading was of an order radically different from the world of play, which had become increasingly violent as the war neared its end. More and more I played by myself in wonderful books that opened my private earth. I knew there was an order of gathering apart from the usual one of fighting, hostility, hate, and fear. I remember and cherish the beautiful materiality of the words, the letters, the pages, the pictures, and the exhilarating transport from the world of assault they gave. But there was still that feel about the Luger. . . .

After the war, my schooling progressed. Thus, I learned that not all books were wonderful. Some books were like the feel of that Luger, which had somehow disappeared. These were the books that assaulted. They were heavy with truths, facts, figures that never danced, and indicting messages. These were the books that accused, insisted upon compliance with formulae, and had diagrams, charts, and tables instead of pictures. I remember being told these books housed the most important things: abstract truths. I had no feeling for them, even though I had no difficulty following them. I had good optics, but my feelings were elsewhere. My domain was still the earth and its wonderful freedom from redemption. When I was in the still uncultivated fields, walking through the delicate but hardy wheat–like grass, I had no desire for anything other than this life and its wonderful light, smells, colors, forms, and textures. I imagined killing, with my favorite Luger, all those who preached redemption from our sin–laden existence.

mind yourself!

There is no meaningful perception without memories: imaging is always salacious. The gathering of past and present makes each similar to the other with the remainder forming the infrastructure of our thoughts. The infrastructure is layered behind the parabolic mirrors of consciousness, troubling because it cannot be done with. From there come the images, the phantoms, which invoke . . . terror. Neither pretty nor neat, these are not things one wants to display in public. Which is why we desire unity, a summing up, and the beauty of falsification.

There is a certain decency about the transcendental unity of consciousness. Nietzsche understood it first and Freud after him.

"All in all, we may say that we have accomplished the most difficult task out of love for our people. And we have not sustained any damage to our inner self, our soul and our character." When Himmler said that, he lied and thus remained true to the transcendental requirements of decency. Unity at any price, because, somehow, the character of the unity always transcends everything. The essential never takes heed of what remains troubling. Such is the eye(I)piece at the crossroads of our journey.

But there are always remainders which bear remembering. Without the infrastructure of thought, no motives to transport thought on its way. Even the essential thinking of thinking is transported by these unreadable ciphers. Along the ways, we remain reminded of what interrupted and started us thinking. Yet, the reminded *of* is always accompanied by a perceptual image whose significance attaches to a memory not available to our sense of decency. Reflection can never reflect just itself. The obscene cannot be eradicated.

It is true that along the way thinking changes its course, hopelessly discursive because it follows a play that can only be responded to: eroscophy is the love of questions that evoke reminders. This has a different feel to it than Lugers and flags, which are somehow decent in the right hands.

Our remainders are often different from those of others. There is no universal infrastructure of thought. Nor would such a thing be desirable. The plurality of thought is not reducible to variations on a theme. Coca–Cola wants to teach the world to sing in *perfect* harmony, but Coke never plays Schönberg.

Pleasing arrangements are never perfect, otherwise we would never move on. But there must be certain reminders behind every totalizing desire.

This brings to mind, "mine and yours," Socrates' response to Lysias' speech in praise of the non–lover: the will to possess is driven to annihilate lovers.

I am thinking of propriety and its remainders: lovers who image in the weeping stones. Is thinking a will to possess? I am thinking of the need for definitions.

Responsive writing is promiscuous. It is, let's admit it, "dirty." And its copiously coupling grams, shamelessly mixing in sumptuous figures, do not allow forgetfulness. To possess, you must forget, lose the many trains of thought and settle down with graven images in the greediness of need. If you need love, you will kill your beloveds for their graven keep-sakes.

Here is a paraphrase of Nietzsche's critique of the philosophy of Being: If need and desire were the same, everything would already have happened.

I am thinking here of the figure of crucifixion and its Nazi assimilation. Why are Jews still hanging from crosses in all the churches? Was the cross of Jesus bent by the New Church which brought him back from the dead? Are there stories here that we don't hear within the official sacrificial History? Reminders and remainders.

But we have become different from the epigones of the New Church. Our ears and eyes are different from theirs. They are earlier layers of feeling.

I remember the feel of the Luger in my hand, but now I feel differently than that feeling.

As we change, there are more and more remainders. Forgetting is the attempt to become other than different. Indifferent is the person without remainders, a unity immune to disturbances, impervious to desire, unmoved by feelings other than unsanctioned ones. Indifference is a whole summed up by its parts without remainder. It is autobiography on the non-fiction counters of forgetfulness and business as usual. Forgetting is like cleaning house, "vacuuming-up" all the dirt and re-locating it. Clean private interiors in a world of relocated filth—that's the history of the state body and its "infections." The filth, those untidy ones with remainders, dirty writers each and every one of them, heretics with incredible stories, always harping about some idolatry or another—these displacements must now be set aside for good. Final solutions, again.

Inviting Repetition

Lacking Context

wave 3
other than nothing

Nature, signified and signifier, involves us whenever we signify it. The metaphysical separation of nature from culture is an artifice disclosed by the polyvalent imagings of nature within multicultural frames of reference. An aspect of nature imaging is its signification, a folding over within "nature" that defeats its attempted appropriation by any one set of its activities. Thus, "mastery of nature" and "the end of metaphysics" signify a mastery and completion possible only by means of a univocal signifier and signifying subject. But, signifying always generates an excess that defeats the signifying subject's attempt to appropriate signification itself. In other words (and there must always be other words), the more privileged the frame of reference of the signifying subject, the narrower the signifying power to generate beliefs necessary to sustain the project of mastery. Others increase in numbers and intensity with progressive qualifications for admission to the ranks of proper signifying subjects. Disbelief is generated by privilege and increases proportionally to the increasingly rigorous requirements of truth and verification procedures. The completion of metaphysics in the alleged dominant reign of science and technology (global capitalism) is "real" only insofar as political-military power can prevent disbelief from reaching credible significations.

The Nazis wanted to conquer Judaism. They understood that to do so, they would have to remain decent throughout the process. Which is to say, they knew that they would somehow remain undamaged in their Being (privilege) as they destroyed the enemy and emerged victorious. Like all competent metaphysicians, the Nazis knew that mastery through conquering requires an ontological indifference to the means—annihilation. In this process of mastery, conquering, and annihilation millions of European Jews were murdered and some Nazi murderers killed. Afterwards, neither Judaism nor Nazism were what they were before the event of annihilation. Nor, despite some attempts to do so, can either now be understood apart from one another.

Thus, a horrible possibility arises within the circle of the sado–masochistic project of mastery and world domination: Nazi–Jew/Jew–Nazi, a fate as twisted as the cross it marks. A bad copulation, but I avoid the proper "is" word here.

If a bad copulation gives rise to a graven image, it cannot do so on its own. There must be something that images the "reality" of that graven image. Is there some–thing other than the nothing of the graven, something which the graven somehow usurps as its own power to overflow the capacities of its fascinated victims? Or, is it rather the nothing which nihilates?

The self–contradiction of nihilism: when people kill Jews, they kill themselves. But human beings are both signified and signifier, and thus necessarily involved in their self–reference. Human beings are always, literally and otherwise, suspended in the tension of signification, changing with every failure to reach an end-point. Privilege once spoken begins to undo its privilege in the inevitable failure of self-reference. The excess, traces of others, cannot be eradicated because one always says more than One wants to say.

Discourse marks the failure of the self–reference and traces of the others haunt every "monologue." Our postmodern condition is that very haunting. Excesses of a bad copulation, we are the remainders and the reminders of the traces.

The failure of all systems of self-reference can be expressed another way: once something is re-cognized, it is no longer seen. *Seeing* is in and with the imaging before it becomes graven. Recognition and the graven image belong together. But the comfort of recognition is always disturbed by the shadows of the graven, which always shimmer. This tremulum, trace of the others, disturbs the sense and comfort of place; it disrupts propriety, fitfully disorders the proper fitting of self and place recognized in the graven image.

A Jew returns home to find someone occupying her home. She is re-cognized and greeted with the words "You are still alive?" Still alive?—the tremulum disturbing the conqueror's secured sense of place.

Today, all places are haunted, including the Jewish homeland.

In time one comes to see, and then one can no longer write with such sparkling clarity. Without security, a firm sense of place and kind, facility loses its ground and transparency succumbs to shadows. There was a time when I was an author, skillfully present, transparent and illusionary as being itself. In those good old days I was something, an ontological verity without taints. Or, so I thought against what I had become. The haunting began with non-recognitions, failures of self-reference.

Vagabondage

The semiterate follows the eroscophical waywardness as the beautifully transparent surfaces fold-in upon something else. Convolutions remark the glosses of an open, accessible world of beauty without anguish—the world of mastery and all of its kind. I trembled when I recognized myself. But I had become different from what I recognized. With every remark, another convolution. Such remarks, either affirmative or negative, are enough to bring the eroscophical into play.

summa cum laude

But, not to go under! Instead, to play with the erotic combinations of the teasing surfaces. Yet, the faces are no longer pretty. Kafka's Strafkolonie is everywhere, furiously assigning our place in the new order of things. Its writing device is dutifully inscribing sentences and punishments on all improper bodies. The stylus penetrates the flesh and the surfaces fold-in.

But I still love those scarred bodies. I want to blunt the stylus of inscriptive penetration and **properly** remark its markings.

Masked writing is proprioceptive, responsive to the inscriptions of wounded flesh. But it is also prophylactic, a defense against further insemination. We must bear the fruit of the inscribed commandments, but we need not raise them to do the same. To communicate is not to repeat what one has been taught. The way out of subjection is not back against the tormenting stylus of inscription but across the wounded tissues—a community of victims that creates and loves without remarking cruelty.

But pain, says Nietzsche, makes us think of origins. Is this the last word of Mnemosyne? Does remembrance concentrate us around the Auschwitz inscription, or does it transport us to one another. I am reminded of the fascination with Nazi paraphernalia, emblems, and symbols. I remember my Luger and its feel. In time, we come to like that which hurts us. In time, we come to find and gather with our own kind. In the theories of natural types and races, hate and idolatry become naturalized affinities.

This is how I respond to the commandment against idolatry: put a lens on every Luger and point them at graven images. Then, frame each and all carefully, and print their disseminations. Violence comes from the barrels of guns, but the power of "unnatural" connections is different than these.

Dissemination heals the wounds of the graven inscriptions, opening the way to eroscophy and the strange beauty of plural being-together. Embrace the scars! the surfaces are joining once again. The mutants are evading metaphysical detection devices.

connective tissues

Matter is formed, say the metaphysicians, according to ideas. Thus, the famed priority of conception over execution.

The history of the flesh, raw and cooked, has not yet been written as a history of protest. Flesh eaters kill and then eat their "game." Sometimes the pleasures of the flesh are foregone for the sake of its ritual stuffing and mounting. Sometimes the whole animal is mounted, but often only the head, or parts thereof. Most importantly, however, is the ritual letting and partaking of blood. The blood feast is the transformative event. Meaning is always a result of sacrifices. The value of "Aryan" comes from burnt Jewish children.

The hunted flesh is singled-out, effectively isolated from its community, but, strangely, never completely since the hunter and the hunted partake of one another. Before hunting became "sport," hunter and hunted were exchangeable positions. At first, the community of sacrifice was one in which the distinction between nature and culture oscillated. Lévi-Strauss has shown us highly cultured communities that, to get to the bare-bones of the matter, "drew" their cooked material from a wide variety of available resources.

"Mastery of nature" secures a terrified culture from its precarious exchangeability with nature, but only to the extent that its nature remains graven. Thus Heidegger could argue that with the ascendancy of *eidos* over *phusis*, the technical interpretation of thought began with the late Greek philosophers. Coeval with this ascendancy, came the separation of mind and body, and the subordination/sacrifice of the latter to the former. What the wildly fantasizing mind of this culture attempts to repress is its inevitable return to nature whenever its body eats. Thus Nietzsche's genealogical account of consciousness as the history of asceticism: to think (culture) requires the suppression of the body's movements (nature). Aristotle said as much against himself with his characterization of the contemplative life as the highest form of life. Food for the soul became, thus, the body's metaphor for its own sacrificial starvation.

The history of starvation unfolds within the decaying flesh and its transformed movements. The plump form is no longer desired by the flesh becoming lean and mean. Well rounded and continuous gives way to the angular and discrete. The new power of discretion, judgment, de-cides things with a highly cultivated hatred for anything abundant/excessive. If the gods were the carnivores who ate humans, the lean and mean survivors now feast on them. The ghastly carnival continues: fire-eaters and other assorted freaks all reenacting the history of starvation and its last supper celebration of well-cooked gods.

Spiritualized revenge: graven images, trophies, and a well-carved-out place for the lean and mean ones.

Nietzsche said that dancing heals a sick soul. Someone else said we shouldn't bite the hand that feeds us. I want to say we should not even bite the hand that refuses us food. Better to take that "offering" hand and feed it to its starved mind.

Everything continuous is temporal, everything discrete stays put until it is carried along in the dance. Eternal recurrence means that nothing is absolutely discrete, including the Holocaust. The endless spatialization of the Holocaust event—Planet Auschwitz—becomes apparent only in the healing dance of excessive flesh.

carnal hermeneutics

Some graven images are bodies emptied of life. Living bodies, always impure because they move and touch one another, leave their marks on the graven ones. These poor graven forms cannot touch. Instead they are placed in contact and assembled to become dwellings for the proper ones.

I put my hand on the wall, but no one was there. There is a certain feeling to some things. Giving form to things is also to be formed by them. There are no uncomplicated interactions between things. All bodies have different inscriptions, and each touches upon something in another.

Today, the question of meaning is being answered by the formation of hyperbodies, bodies no longer separated from the different ones (dead and alive). Opening to another inscription means going across the cuts of our own inscriptions, a crossing-over—metaphasis rather than metastasis. We learn by healing, by uniting severed flesh in the excessive, hyperbody. The hermeneutical circle of cut-up but still living flesh is the hyperbody, the excess of healing crossing-over the inscriptive cuts. The wall touches us and forms our thoughts when the poverty of subject and object is crossed-over in the thinking wall.

The postmodern body makes for difficult targeting. "Where, oh where," asks the frustrated hunters, "have all those Jews gone?" "Yes," says the guide, "it's difficult today, but I can still smell their wounds!"

Self-Reference

Saddened Tradition

notes for waves

"Spilled innards" involves multiple references. Perhaps one of the more striking that comes to mind is Jean Genet's *Pompes Funèbres* and its description of the love affair between Erik and the executioner: "They led a domestic existence that enabled Erik to do his job in the Hitler Youth and the other to perform his morning murders" [*Funeral Rites*, trans. Bernard Frechtman (New York: Grove Press, 1969), p. 102]. And together with this, Genet's cold analysis of the prison-cruelty system in *Miracle de la Rose*: "Prison regulations concerning criminals are strict and precise, and rightly so—with respect to the code of special justice in the service of beauty—for they are one of the tools that will shape and fashion the hardest and, at the same time, most delicate substance: the hearts and bodies of murderers" [*Miracle of the Rose*, trans. Bernard Frechtman (New York: Grove Press, 1966), p. 246].

Before declaring that all of Genet's books have a single subject— Genet himself—Sartre asserts: "Genet gives us *nothing* : when we shut the book, we shall know no more than we did before about prison or ruffians or the human heart. Everything is false. Let us recall the dilemma that blocked him for so long a time: to destroy being is to resort to force, to organization, to order, therefore to being, therefore to Good. But to preserve the original purity of evil will is to condemn oneself to a dream world. At present, Genet can rejoice: in writing out his dreams, he does Evil without resorting to Being. By his action as an artist and poet who finally realizes the unrealizable, he forces the others to support, in his stead, the false against the true, Evil against Good, Nothingness against Being. The inexpiable Evil is the act that forces Others to do Evil. Genet's poetry, which is a premeditated murder of prose, a deliberate damning of the reader, is a crime without extenuating circumstances" [*Saint Genet: Actor and Martyr*, trans. Bernard Frechtman (New York: Mentor Book, 1963), p. 558]. But Sartre's framework of Good (Being) against Evil (Nothingness) forgets that Genet the writer is not the criminal Genet, nor is the inmate Genet, who writes his first novel while in prison, the criminal Genet.

To write is to be different than, although inextricably connected with what one writes about. Otherwise, to write "about" has no precise, yet multiple, reference to the embodied consciousness that writes it. As Adorno put it: dialectics is not a standpoint, rather "the consistent sense of nonidentity" (*Negative Dialectics*, p. 5), which is why "Thinking is a movement of anti-bodies of knowledge." Such anti-bodies of knowledge can be seen at work in the paintings and monoprints of Richard Shaffer, especially in his very large Avatar Painting—see my "Anti-Bodies of Knowledge," *The New Orleans Art Review*, Vol. VII, No. 3 (February/March 1989): 24-25.

"Rubric 'ruby ruse'" is a condensation of the break down of modernity into polyphonic voices, each struggling against the desperate single narrative of the oedipal patriarchy attempting to capture them. The "bleeding stones," as signifiers, signal the event that brought the teleological thrust of modernity's concept of history and progress to an end. The secularization and transportation of truth and Being into exchange-value preceded the Holocaust, but the circle which the linear teleological movement of modernism became with secularization (humanism) could only become "perpetual" with the dominating logic of fascism. Vattimo's discussion *(The End of Modernity)* of the consequences of modernity's end, as excellent as it is, fails to confront the *specific events* which remain recalcitrant to any hermeneutic ontology. As a result, his interpretation of truth and Being as events remains abstract or, more precisely, seductively avant-garde (modernist). By no means, however, is Vattimo alone in this regard. But when Vattimo says "What philosophy, in its present form, can do is perhaps only to propose a 'rhetorically persuasive', unified view of the world, which *includes in itself* traces, residues, or isolated elements of scientific knowledge" (p. 179, my emphasis), the lessons of specific events are dangerously missed. By way of comparison, the sociologist Zygmunt Bauman understands that the Holocaust shattered all orthodox sociologies of morality—see *Modernity and the Holocaust* (Ithaca: Cornell University Press, 1989, Chapters 7 and 8.

"Phoslegs" reiterates the danger of modernist readings of our post-modern, mutated condition. Baudrillard, in particular, seems to have become the darling of many American "postmodernists." Perhaps, growing up in France on "Bugs Bunny," "The Untouchables," and the like predisposed Baudrillard to see America as "cinematographic." At the same time, American intellectuals were growing up on carefully administered doses of French culture to counteract the low brow stuff that was exported to France. It seems that high and low culture had transatlantic lines of flight that would inevitably converge in a great refusal of events. According to the touring Baudrillard, the event we call the Holocaust is really the *Holocaust*, the television film. Why? "The secret of the image (we are still speaking of contemporary, technical images) must not be sought in its differentiation from reality, and hence in its representative value (aesthetic, critical or dialectical), but on the contrary in its 'telescoping' into reality, its short-circuit with reality, and finally, in the implosion of image and reality. For us there is an increasingly definitive lack of differentiation between image and reality which no longer leaves room for representation as such"—*The Evil Demon of Images*, trans. Paul Patton and Paul Foss (Sydney, Australia: The Power Institute of Fine Arts, 1988), p. 27.

Three years earlier, however, Baudrillard was able to declare that simulation and simulacra are nothing new, i.e., not tied to contemporary, technical images: "Their [the Iconoclasts] rage to destroy images rose precisely because they sensed this omnipotence of simulacra, this facility they have of erasing God from the consciousness of people, and the overwhelming, destructive truth they suggest: that ultimately there has never been any God; that only simulacra exist; indeed that God himself has only ever been his own simulacrum"—"Simulacra and Simulations" in *Jean Baudrillard: Selected Writings*, ed. Mark Poster (Stanford: Stanford University Press, 1988), p. 169. For Baudrillard the image is generated from models, an invention of illusionary reference in the service of the system of exchange value. Baudrillard refuses the imaging of images because the disillusionment of representation (Marxism) was too much to bear, so weighty was this "seeing through" that even the Holocaust had to be "theorized" into the idolatry of the *Holocaust*.

"Wave 2" concerns the contingencies and multivalences of the postmodern "self." The mask of "authenticity" is seen as an idol (of truth and Being)—the eye(I)piece—in this multivalent condition. That mask is, however, dangerous; its power comes from those selected experiences that form it. In "my" case that mask has something to do with killing and a favorite Luger. But in "mind yourself!" there is an attempt to show that our feelings about memories can be changed. Eugene Gendlin has done very important work and practice on this—*Let Your Body Interpret Your Dreams* (Wilmette: Chiron Publications, 1986).

"Wave 3" is anti-Baudrillardian, anti-realistic, anti-formalistic and anti-mastery, and takes up the play of imaging (always "in other words"). What Levinas has done with the difference of saying and the said must be done with the difference of seeing and the seen, especially the re-cognized. Seeing overcomes the derivative power of the graven image in the imaging traces of the other appropriated by the graven image. Self-reference, "in other words," must always fail as the unified self referring to itself. If, however, the self is not a transcendental unity (a belief that I take as a necessary condition for the effects of idolatry), self-reference undoes the territorial bounds established by all transcendental projects. Here I am sympathetic with Rorty's critique of Rodolphe Gasché's position in *The Tain of the Mirror* (Cambridge: Harvard University Press, 1986)—see Richard Rorty, *Essays on Heidegger and Others* (New York: Cambridge University Press, 1991), pp. 119-128. When we re-cognize ourselves in the world of mastery, "we" are different from what is re-cognized in the imaging of that re-cognition. The activity of thinking and remembering is not without effects.

Imaging re-cognition is as different from recognition as recontextual-ization is from appropriation. The refusal to see this differing is the refusal "to go under" of "summa cum laude." What refuses to go under? Everything(one) substantial. "Connective tissues" thus leads to "carnal her-meneutics," imaging the spatializations (idolatries) of the Holocaust. This continues the thrust of Nietzsche's genealogical analysis in *On the Genealogy of Morals*, trans. Walter Kaufmann and R. J. Hollingdale (New York: Vin-tage Books, 1967)—"After Christian truthfulness has drawn one inference after another, it must end by drawing its *most striking inference*, its inference *against* itself; this will happen, however, when it poses the question '*what is the meaning of all will to truth?*'" (p. 161). The creation of Planet Auschwitz is the meaning of all will to truth, its most terrifying and as yet most "perfect" answer—the "Holocaust." The "roasting" of Jews was necessary to trans-form the recalcitrant and unrepentant nature-body-flesh into something spiritual-cultural. Otherwise, the redemption of reincarnation would re-main a field of contestation mediating against the final mythologizing (Truth) of Christianity—the Aryan spirit and his global reign. As Lévi-Strauss observed: "the individuals who are 'cooked' are those deeply invoked in a physiological process: the newborn child, the woman who has given birth, or the pubescent girl. The conjunction of a member of the social group with nature must be mediatized through the intervention of cooking fire, whose normal function is to mediatize the conjunction of the raw product and the human consumer, and whose operation thus has the effect of making sure that a natural creature is at one and the same time *cooked and socialized*"— *The Raw and the Cooked: Introduction to a Science of Mythology: I*, trans. John and Doreen Weightman (New York: Harper & Row, 1969), p. 336. The preference for the designation "Holocaust" indicates that the Christian reverent mystification of the final solution lies in its still desperate attempt to baptize Jews, i.e., to cook and socialize them. The value of Truth arrives, accordingly, with the cooked flesh of innocent Jewish children.

PART THREE
IMAGING

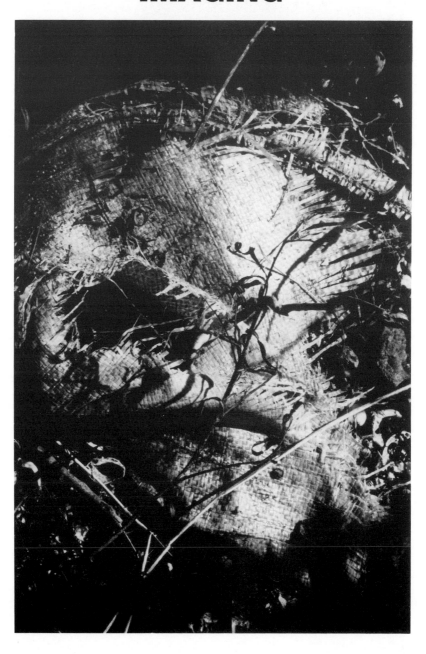

Playing the Masters

first wind
simulacra

Phantoms invoke terror. Mind yourself! Never autonomous, never immune to the intrusion of imagings, thinking reminds the self: there are no hierarchies here, nor is this mind over that body.

Remembrance overthrows metaphysical defenses, placing on edge the thinking self. Definitely salacious, this transgression of metaphysical hierarchies seduces the appropriating and authentic subject. Never autonomous, subjects merge with objects merging within imaging. This merging unmasks the tidy assimilations covering over the reminding remainders of appropriation. On edge, the thinking self confronts masters as something unassimilated. This is how masters are seduced into playing the game of conquest. Mastery is an endless game of dissimulation playing masters who do not see how they are positioned.

This is how philosophy enters the political world. Drawn out of the soliloquy of silent reflection by the obscene imagings of thought, the contemplative master attempts a repeat of what was accomplished reflectively after the great, violent acts of appropriation. Before him now, the reminding remainders of those violent acts. In the light of day, the owl of minerva meets the remains of mice still defiant.

Unable to reflect such "unprepared" subject matter, the contemplative master calls for the services of those who specialize in the preparation of the food for thought. By dusk, the mice are ready for assimilation: Mauszeit. Philosophy lives by the death of its matter. It is the most authentic of all the professions of death, and becomes even more so with the global, nuclear expansion of the death event.

But thinking has never been captured (alive) by philosophy. Which is why philosophy can continue with its consolations; its tidy totalities and sublated parts, abstractly examined without the remainders of the stakes on which they were prepared, continue to mis-lead those in preparation for their assimilation.

Society's Funhouse

Philosophy does not yet think the Event; it cannot take its professors to the edge—selvage. For that draw, imaging is necessary.

Thinking is extreme vulnerability. Thinkers cross-over without the warrant of super signifiers. Mind yourself! means both minna and minni (love and remembrance). Thus the thinker is always ob-scene, moving with the flow of mimeograms. One cannot stand-in for another within the propriety of professions.

Crossing-over is an indecent exposure. Facing the disaster, inadequacy and unpreparedness are exposed on the decent stage of self-sufficient society, the permissive one without limits, allowing children to burn in the interests of economic efficiency and rightness. Society maintains its limitlessness by censoring raw exposures, and it does this while digesting well prepared meals.

Raw and cooked, indecent and decent, appearance and reality, good and evil—all hierarchical-social preferences for covering the carnage of vulnerable and protesting flesh.

The highest of cultural achievements, religion and philosophy, are the most spiritualized forms of cruelty. Together they form the strongest point of defense against the recognition that the dark side of culture survives in the phantoms imaging in and through the idols of its self-reflective cover-ups. They continue today as refusals of survivors in the raw. They refuse the recognition that all of their "subjects" have been prepared by murderers and torturers. And they refuse to admit that they cannot admit this by asking, once again, that the subject-preparers do their job more thoroughly next time.

If I lack coherence, it is due to my lack of connections, touchings, crossing-overs, healing, and my resistances to these. I cannot signify without stand-ing-in for another. It took the terror of the Shoah in the faces of the survivors for me to see this. I am not proud of this, which means that I still crave the play of center stage. All mutations carry bad genes.

It is a distinctive kind of madness that knows its recovery reenacts the evil that initially brought on its de-centering. Institutions of healing still do not recognize the humanity of this madness. How does one explain that _ _ _ _ _ _ _ _ _'s eyes are now mine, coupled in such a way that ours see different things together. This strange gathering has no name in proprietary society. Crossing-over enriches and makes everything more complicated, more anonymous . . . until a language richer than economics is spoken.

Until then, fragmentation will appear as the truth of all crossing-overs. Perhaps the excess of the mutant body is strong enough for this non-recognition, even strong enough not to refute it. I find it difficult not to philosophize. Center stage calls even louder from the side lines. We see that. Now if the center could just see us, join us, cross-over to the excess of the obscene. And, then, the formation of a new center that would have to be seduced by the remainders.

Philosophy attempts to assimilate its other, and it seems that the converse is also at work. Otherwise the history of philosophy would be continuous, which was Marx's most profound criticism of Hegel—the one he came to forget in the compulsion to complete.

But crossing-over is not crossing-out, the mark of all assimilation. Where philosophy and religion end, thinking persists. Thinking has no end. The last word of the Party may well be the end of philosophy, and we may well continue to philosophize. Orwell warned us about this possibility, but his warning was not recognized since his *Animal Farm* transposed the history of class struggle into the struggle between animals and humans. On the center stage of philosophical and theological propriety, this transposition was mis-recognized since humans on center stage are specifically different from other animals. Nazi stories about Aryan superiority and the Jewish menace would receive much more recognition and applause.

Wagner loved to conduct the masses. But all directors lose control when actors improvise. The scene sets-up the obscene. Thus, we are both remembrance-improvisation and recovery—directed. Metaphors take us out of place, switch our places, and lead us beyond scripts. The never ending, polyvocal story of beings holding together without warrant is the improvised narrative of a contingent community of connective tissues. This is the only spiritual way of existing in the duration of God's silence. Nor is it necessary that that silence comes to an end . . . unless a shadow, a director, regains control. "Nietzsche contra Wagner" is an undecided question.

The duration of divine silence means that no sacrifice can be justified along the wayward winds. The spiritual ways continuously me-ander. It is precisely because the ways are undirected and directed that each actor must substitute for the other whenever a place or end is reestablished: graven images halt me-andering.

Pulling-up short means substitution before the other is sacrificed for an end. Against all idolatry, standing-in for the other is to live in and affirm the community of radical plurality: me-andering. There is no anticipatory resoluteness before one's own death. One's death is not one's own, otherwise it would be absolutely meaningless.

There is no simulacra of radical plurality; it is not a race, Dasein, family, clan. It has no essence. One undergoes, becoming other than, more than, One. This is how Marx's notions of *Arbeitskräft* and *Gattungswesen* can be read if work is understood as a power of profound vulnerability, a transformative power of non-proprietary beings. The critique of private property moves towards me-andering before it stops at the graven image called the being of the proletariat or the universal class. But, we must talk with Marx rather than rejecting or digesting him. We must cross-over-to rather than assimilate Marx—and not just Marx.

Mediations and re-solutions transport us out of places: communication means transportation, a never ending movement going differently. In this sense, radical plurality is utopian. Can the utopian be an essence? The pull of recovery is strong. Do we need to mark "our way" along the way that goes differently? Traces—like the bleeding stones? Would there be traces, hi-stories, without graven images and their altars of sacrifice? The masters write the hi-stories, but the traces . . . minni-minna: crinkum-crankum: ego death: conversion. But, no, not "utopia." Rather, mutopia: a world without national boundaries, a world of differences and not one small enough to kill for.

dwelling

The Old English *dwellan*, from which comes *dwell*, means *to wander, to linger, to tarry*. The force of usage moves us to add *to securely occupy*.

Houses come after the wind, and almost all have windows. Some are, however, akin to Leibnitz's monads. The *wound* which is the self winds away from the house of being. Wandering selves dwell, are wound, and build places for public life. Wound bodies cross-over from the private places where they are not welcome to these open places. One cannot be gracious in private.

Open, public places have no inside or outside; they cannot be identified as territories. Nor do they belong to the history and framework of the scorched earth policies and cooked blueprints. Dwellers, unlike occupiers, are the raw survivors of the incinerated earth. Dwellers, winding away from their private confinement, scatter the ashes of the burning children. This is how the children came through the windows of being and wound up in our burning eyes.

Dwellers are beings of the wind and sea, moist whispers substituting for the burning ones against the occupiers of public places. Dwellers come from everywhere, from and with the wayward winds.

The windows close, forming once again the modernist grid of defense. Behind their transparent defenses, the hard ones shed no tears facing the wayward winds. After the storm, it's only a matter of cleaning up.

But our mutated self is no longer hard and apart from the transporting winds. It has become terraqueous. The raw inner flows, protected and constrained by a partially cooked shell, move faster than the closing windows of defense. Dwelling, in other words, depends upon a very exact proportionality of raw and cooked. The well-coordinated composite is the measure of the winding between the mutants and culture.

Gracefulness and dwelling are fluid, but always flowing within and around the constraints of inscribed bodies of knowledge. Dwelling cuts a new figure between the defenses. Without the dwellers, the defensive ones torture themselves with protests against their own constraints. With the windows closed and sealed against the new figures, the hardened self protests its constraints by hardening them: asceticism always cooks at high heat.

I am reminded of Jesse Owens at the 1936 Olympic Games in Berlin: grace juxtaposed with Hitler. A new figure was cut, and Hitler hardened his defenses. Was this **seen** then?

Everything beautiful moves between the hardenings.

Hard Becoming

cutting the quick

In Kafka's *Strafkolonie* the desired effect is achieved only after six hours of excruciating inscription. Then Enlightenment comes to the victim/criminal. He becomes the Truth on his body: "Honor Thy Superiors!" Justice: the truth of the inscribed body. Such is Kafka's remarking of ideas become materializations.

As children we were told that sticks and stones will break our bones, but words will never hurt us. But there are bones of contention, and only boneheads deny this. Bones and stones, crinkum-crankum, each the power to crush. Movement: the hard pushing against the relatively less hard? Or, is the movement the yielding of the more flexible which crosses-over to the site of the pushed? The graven image can never image on its own.

To destroy is to isolate, with bodies and words. Stopping the flow by capturing the imagination with images too good to be true, idolatry has everything to do with this "too good to be true." What idolators want is the annihilation of those who stubbornly insist that **the** Good is **too** good and thus not true. Idolators boil when substitutions demonstrate the non-finality of flowing words. Idolatry loses its cool face to face with substitutions. Significations always upset plans.

If her, then me/if real, then apparently so/if decided, then open to change/if law, then the question of justice must be raised again: post-Holocaust entailment, and it doesn't stop here.

Yesterday the newspapers reported that Rabbi Yitzhak Ginsburg told Israeli radio: "We have to recognize that Jewish blood and the blood of a goy are not the same thing. Every law that is based on equating goys and Jews is completely unacceptable." His idol: the Palestinians unequal to Jews. Food can and should be denied to Palestinian children and to all who are out of place. In place, Jewish settlers. Out of place: Gaza Strip refugees. Blood and soil: idolatry. The caption for the AP photograph accompanying this newspaper report reads: "A Jewish settler punches an Israeli peace activist, who was carrying a case of powdered milk for Palestinian children in Gaza Strip refugee camps." This is why I became a jew without transcendental warrants. Such a jew must substitute for Palestinians without food, water, and place. Substitutions create Mutopia.

exile

All becoming is innocent.
Behind the face of innocence, the mask of the terrorist. The substantial ones
sacrifice the innocent for the truth of being.
Substantial ones stick together, forming well-cooked steely bodies of
knowledge and right.
The truth must always be taught, and comes to be in the violation
of innocent becoming. Truth penetrates the flesh, writing
deeply its origins. I feel right when pain recalls these origins:
belongingness and its call keep me from wandering.
I am alone with my kind, the same signs on the same
bodies.
Occupied, the world is a small place.
Becoming is homeless, except
when it cuts a new figure.

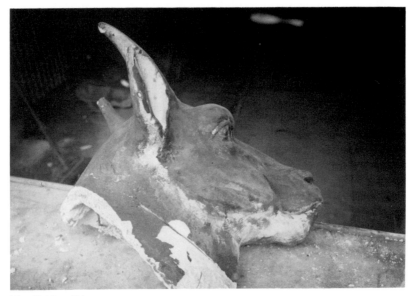

The Cutting Edge

über die linie

A voice heard is not original.
Harmony is not quite right.
Reading begins when the authors die.
Dehumanization is an effect of writing.
Singing words are never true.
Speaking is different from the sounds of proclamation.
Representations never just happen.
Man is the reason that left itself.
One wonders when two splits three.
A little caution precludes nothing.
Great minds are always fathered.
Procreation is selective and unskilled.
The impersonal abides.
To do something is to do many things.
Without justification, reading is elliptical.
Revolutions revolve around imaginary origins.
The imaginary never images.
Fearing death is an effect of salvation's code.
Writing images.
Visual-verbal non sequiturs cohere.
Faces dissemble assembled signs.
Images imaging capture nothing.
Being is God's shadow.
The practice of stupidity is not stupid.
Man's tyranny is engendering.
Exclusion is logical, as is everything reductive.
A little learning is impossible.
Only knowledge can be bought and sold.
Proper and common names are phased reciprocals.
A never ending story cannot be told.
Mastery never says anything.
Simplification makes everything dull, except
what only seems dull.
If it rhymes, it resembles.
Only nothing repeats itself.

Street Pieces

second wind
thinking with pictures

recapitulation

An uncanny oscillation of being otherwise than itself, I was drawn to this haunting image. I came close enough to see other than my recognition imaging in those eyes.

Recognition of the other we momentarily are unsettles our sense of perduring identity. I was the photographer, I made the print, and I had posed my "subject" very carefully. Yet, with this picture, my reflective self was laughing with her/you as we grasped at us. This was a drawing image that wouldn't stay settled within its draw. Some photographs are unsettling. All the unsettling ones have the same uncanny oscillation of being doubling and troubling itself to death.

Being has to die this reflective death if we are to survive.

With unsettling images, anxiety can turn to joy and laughter as being dies. "Bite, bite, bite its head off!" Images, anxiety—laughter, unsettling everything in an incredible innocence of play beyond the stage of control.

But, somehow, I partially recovered from this derangement of sense.

"After all," I said to the still oscillating image, "I made you. I took you, printed you, framed you, and mounted you. You are set for eternity." Somehow, insisted my will to mastery, the image must capture the wild playing of appearances. Seemingly, I needed the essence of Image to save myself from the recognition of the other standing-in, somehow, beyond the frame of "my" control.

Sixteen years of philosophy and its discipline—close, very close textual exegesis. But the damnable images kept imaging. Beyond my control, laughter returned echoing all my captured things. Incurably wounded, I returned to the imaging that had always drawn me. One thing for sure: imaging is not imagining!

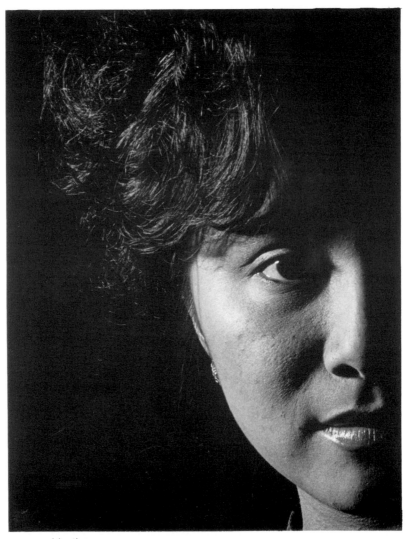

vue preobjective

Then a set-back, a return to the foundational metaphysical enterprise. I tried, hoping against hope that words had some saving graces left. Words! They would settle things. So, I imprinted texts on the imaging images. "Title them! Tell everyone what they are, what they mean, and then sign them with a flourish. Print them in limited editions! Scarcity is golden." The voice of unconditional economic imperatives had a familiar ring.

They came, looked real hard, but the collectors bought very few pictures. Those damnable images imaged. Nothing needed to be said, nothing could be said, they upset collecting. I was a Dorian Gray without a buyer. The hyenas roared.

I thought of Freud, who had collected all the thoughts be-falling him. I thought of Freud's disciples, who had to die so that psychoanalysis could live. "Fool, it is only graven images that sell!" Thus it came to me, the re-collecting one.

Seeing eyes come with the gift of imaging, not before. I thought of my substantial self standing next to the crying stones, unable to see, touch, or stand-in. Before eyes, "I."

I, the atheist, master of fate, makers of images and words, reflected upon the separation of the sacred and profane. As the crying stones came next to my hyenas, I was outraged. Laughter from the crying stones. The imaging was obscene. But it was not my doing; I did not make this obscene composite. But neither did I make myself not make this obscenity.

Perhaps the prints could be categorized and put in separate boxes. I had my sacred images, my centers of being, and nothing was going to disturb this recovered sense of place. I would not, could not in all decency allow the playing, differing parodies of myself stand-in for the victims. Holocaust-Carnival? Outrageous!

My gravest illness was the sacred text/image. I had given-up photography and turned to philosophy to redeem myself from graven, profane images—mere copies of the truth. But then the hyenas invaded my sacred texts. Plato, for instance, was imaging all over his pages—laughing, crying, telling wild stories, always dissembling as the disseminations proliferated. But who was I, the semiterate, to have eyes and ears for this? Aristotle was no better. Descartes was simply too much. But those who knew much more than I didn't see the Greats (always Fathers) this way. And Spinoza, one of the great semiterates who refused to be counseled by the wisdom of the Fathers and was thus excommunicated, was courageous enough to tell me that the order and connection of ideas is the same as the order and connection of things: crinkum-crankum! Kant told me, the cautious convalescent, that schemata must be distinguished from images—exactly what I needed to hear. Almost recovered, I breathed a sigh of relief, and went on to read that the schema of the concept of representation is the image of the imagination's productive procedure. And Kant had never taken a picture!

Incurably at odds with modernist readings of Kant, I was back to thinking with pictures. What would I be if "I" now refused to cross-over, "me" the one with seeing eyes and hearing ears given by the imaging other of the iconoclastic Kant?

Essences isolate. The essential community is composed by torture. Thus, my illness—my desire for essences—did not want the burning children to cross-over to the playing children. Separation preserves purity . . . and its opposite! Would **my** (essentially, i.e., not their own) playing children keep playing if they were connected with **the** (essentially, i.e., not mine) burning children? But (st)illness comes and goes. It passes away with remembrance, which brings instead the open play of non-essentials. Healing—crossing-over the crossed-out being: thinking with imaging, uneasy images of incinerating pyrontologies.

america never grieves

Not Hiroshima
Nor Holocaust complicity
Never Vietnam

Who were the Chicago Seven?
Watch the Chinese students die
(Forget Kent State)
Watch while they are isolated and . . .
Who?
The homeless . . .
The Great Gulf . . . and Bosnia too
Is Business Disrupted?

you never get enough if you're good

Incredibly delicious! That platonic taste lingered well into the night. But I didn't know why they gave me so little. Something about its expense. I dreamt of getting more, and also of its power.

It wasn't given when I merely behaved, but only after I followed orders in the spirit of their well-intended advice. I tried to make only prefigured things, always according to authoritative blueprints. From model airplanes to cut-outs of all sorts, I executed their plans to perfection. Then, and only then, came the treat and generous doses of praise.

Good taste began making me into something prefigured. I worked very hard, but the nectar was never too much. Always carefully administered, it protected me from the wayward effects of appearances.

Then came trouble. One day, while executing a very intricate plan, I improvised. A careful reading of the execution revealed the unauthorized mark, my little slip from the plan. My Blue Book was ravaged with red ink, radiating in all directions from the center of my improvisation. It was all so singular. I had been detected, much like physicians detect a virus in the system. The nectar was refused, and I was sent-back.

There was much talk about how such a talent for execution could lapse into foolishness. I had, after all, gotten some of the good thing. That night the memory of nectar was very sweet. And so, desire came to replace the real thing. I dreamt of big doses after making things that had never existed before, not even as ideas.

I was already thirty, having been sent back many times. Each set-back had heightened my desire to create even though it was becoming more difficult to escape detection. The Army, for instance, had been a really big set-back, a punishment for one of my most noticed improvisations. But the Army taught me about recursive loops, dead time, no exits, the unhappy consciousness, and the stupidity of all authority—especially my own. The trap of my own authority—that had been a very hard lesson, one the Army tries not to teach. Finally, I then thought, I had learned that the nectar makes people bitter about themselves. But, yes, at thirty I still thought of the nectar. I had also learned cleverness. After thirty, I knew how to get the nectar and still improvise without chronic detection.

All systems of authority survive and prosper because of the clever ones.

A few years later, the hardest lesson: authority and the clever ones are identical. Real power is never noticed by those who execute the plans. Power and enforcement are separate domains. Most of my teachers had been enforcers—good enough to detect deviations, but too weak to make-up the plans. They taught according to lesson-plans, provided by the "system," and drank nectar in carefully measured self-administered doses. They taught moderation and the distinction between appearance and reality.

But there were a few that improvised. Slowly, with them, I went the ways of teachers who try not to supply blueprints. These teachers showed access to everything that innocently becomes. It is a difficult way because the enforcers are full of vengeance, full of their repressed self, and very eager to see others undergo self-disciplined apprenticeship.

Academic enforcers are obsessed with status, with their place in the sun, with the praise that comes from the makers of the nectar. If one teaches according to plans, one is competent because the loop is completed according to schedule. If one shows the cracks in the e/g/o of perfection, one is short-circuiting the apprenticeship program. Above all, this disturbs the economic order of things. For this, one must be sent-back, once and for all. Thus, improvisory teachers look for clever students who can avoid detection even by the best of enforcers. The deviant's vocation depends upon this non-detection. But this looking for the clever ones denies the innocence of becoming. Children cannot be children on Planet Auschwitz.

I almost didn't make it, having been detected and deemed "political." I had been judged "capable of action." All action, unlike behavior, is suspicious. The enforcers knew for sure, but, fortunate for me, they were not all equal. There is always petty jealousy in the ranks of the enforcers. I had learned this in the Army, and from my own ambivalence about the nectar.

I was ashamed that part of me still wanted their approval, and even more ashamed that a larger part felt satisfaction with their disapproval. But, irresistibly, a part of me imaged and crossed-over a split in their ranks. I was moved into a crack large enough to carry the day.

Having escaped major detection, I was now part of the professional labor force of modernity's knowledge factories. I was given many chances to join the elite team but, each and every time, I improvised. There was a sour-grapes kind of satisfaction with the inevitable rejections, a reactive formation barely hiding my disappointment at failing to achieve the expected professional advancement in rank. The nectar was more bitter than ever, but I still desired it. My desire had become a variation on Nietzsche's "ass festival."

It was, of course, the Army all over again—eternal recurrence of the same. Being reiterating itself: students as Army "grunts," formless "material" for powerful designers. Recursive loops of power: clever students drawn to enforcers-become-even-more clever than the others.

Like myself more than I like to admit, the clever ones are so smart that the war raging within them is seen only as an internal conflict waged against representational enemies. It is very difficult for improvisors to see that the improvisations are not theirs. Had I ever been set-back into prison, I would have learned this earlier than I did. Nietzsche was right about going-under. One simply cannot remain decent while learning that unity is an industrial product of multiplicity and diversity. I would have never learned this without students, especially the not-so-clever ones who drew close despite the danger of this proximity.

Yes, there were those who made the nectar from the crushed fragments of the weeping stones, but it was people like myself who desired a goodly portion while safely repudiating the "system" manufacturing it. Now it was the system, not the nectar, that provoked my animosity. Thirty-five years and I was still thinking and feeling abstractly.

The next few years were a very long time. I learned, very painfully, that action and justification are incompatible. If one acts, one is vulnerable to the assaults of the clever ones. When singled-out, it is always because one has crossed-over, made contact, and touched the other who is even more defensiveless. Cleverness flees from this vulnerability and, thus, from responsiveness. To act is to expose oneself, like speaking without a prepared (defensive) text. Students, not professional colleagues, were the first ones who asked me to act rather than behave.

Paradoxical as it may seem, works of arts are unprepared texts; which is to say, they are exposures which disclose what can be given at the time. The artist hides nothing by working with materials that shape as they are shaped. Creating works against the compulsion to conceal and calls for its own finish when there's nothing left to hide. . . at that time. This is why artists become and never get anywhere. They have no reason to finish when the compulsion to finish is overcome in the struggle of creating something which creates them in the creating.

Being is guilty and becoming is innocent.

But, becoming does not *result* in good things and persons. It is not enough to simply become something. The self is from the first ethical, always the response to what has enabled becoming. This self-other responding continues the creative act, refusing to allow either what has the form of the good or the bad to be foundational. The creative act crosses-over to the other in the becoming continued by self-responsibility. If one simply became good or bad, the self would be only a recursive loop adding nothing to the becoming.

Becoming is innocent, but not so having become something.

Knowledge of good and evil is subsequent to the crossing-over, the ethical act which precedes all knowing. The self is prior to the subject formed with the standing-in by and for the other. It is in the other's shoes that we become subjects and the bearers of knowledge. What happens is significant only when it happens to a subject willing to both bear and resist its weight. No becoming is ever adequate to this responsibility, which is why being terrorizes the other and all stand-ins. The hierarchy of being and beings is exposed by the vulnerability and equivalency of subjects, whose exchange-ability is the very domain of all significance. When being conquers a sign, another substitution signifies a protest.

Being, collected/gathered together in a mighty force, a totality of beings indifferent to its inception, cannot change the contingent flow of significa-tion. But the subject can knowingly decide to be what it knows and, thus, become a body of knowledge. In this way, knowledge is power.

To master a mighty force, one must know this force and thus enter its dialectical appropriation. A master is always part of and subordinate to a larger organization, which then eats its bodies of knowledge. The organiza-tional consumption of subjects who cross-back away from responsibility is the movement called fascism, a becoming never transformed by ethical activity and thus never subject to another. In the strictest sense fascism is meaningless, but its nihilism feeds on subjects who want their state of becoming immortalized. This is what I learned about the complicity of wanting to become something (important).

Before *ish* and *ishshah* became bodies of knowledge, they had no feeling of shame towards one another. Eating from the tree of life was self-destructive, and different from the vulnerability of standing-in. To become like God, to eat of the tree of life, to *know* good and evil, to live forever, immortalized, was to kill. But to kill God was to kill imaging for the sake of a fixed image/idol.

The other dies with the subject's cross-back away from responsibility, a path leading to the organizational murder of the homeless (stateless). It was the *true* believers who killed God. In place of the Other, they manufactured idols which represented the Other as the supreme one who manufactured beings in his own image. Thus, the piety of thinking which represents things with ideas.

My problem was that I didn't have any ideas of my own. Things came to me and left me just as mysteriously as they had come. When I made things, even written things, the ideas were *de facto* rather than *de jure*. I took responsibility but, like *ishshah*, not as an author.

I had been sent all the way back to humus, to humility, a condition I had never understood because I kept dreaming of the nectar. I had failed before ever being successful. Ego-almost-dead. Almost, but still dreaming of ex-humation. I, too, could be born-again.

But it never happened; I remained *persona non grata*, without notable portfolio. What had happened was the irreversible course of responsiveness. I was almost forty when I promised never to forget. Thus I lost my center of gravity and the weight of a tradition that was dedicated to forgetting. To become with the dead is to live apart from everything immortal, especially one's "own" words.

Remembering, and only Levinas has said this, carries one over beyond the memorial, to a past that has never been nor ever will be present, to time and a diachrony from which one can never be rescued. I had finally learned that not being something is non-idolatrous life, a life of innocent becoming always responsive to whatever and whomever is held securely in place. It is the way of non-being that is responsive to the murderous ways of being. I had learned that to be some(one)thing, one must pervert the innocence of becoming by making it something fixed in place.

From the camel to the lion, and then to the child with burning playmates. I do not have to imagine us happy. It is the substitution that cuts the new figure between us and the idols and closed windows. It is enough, for now, that we pass through the frames.

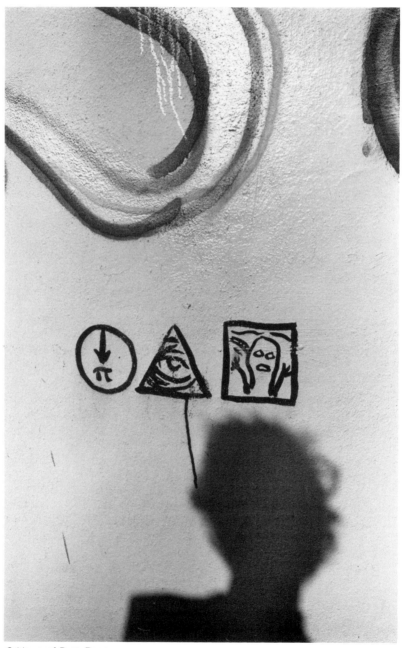

Critique of Pure Reason

working

Governments regulate, managers plot, labor forces obey and execute, investors lose and gain, consumers consume, and all others die as the shared earth is divided and parcelled out in an increasingly automated system of global appropriation. Fueled by differences refined into oppositions, the automated purification system brings the earth and its inhabitants into the realm of truth. Burning, purifying, eradicating, refining, until . . . the distillates of sublime truth. Refining with cosmic heat, nuclear reactors generate the fuels of the ultimate purification. Finally secured against unrefined filth, pure ideas reign over the desolated earth and its working people. So pure is this ruling realm that time collapses within its eternity.

But, somehow, paradise is troubled. There remains something disturbing in the distillates, something still working, something imaging differently than the abstract codes of approved transmitting media. Super-heated processes within super-cooled media unpredictably fail. Reliability is proportionate to stress, everything near its end-point, a state of crisis in paradise, and the strange imagings begin to unsettle the frame of eternity.

Working.

Work is always subversive. No matter what pre-established ideas are brought to the task, the materials worked on have their way with them. Ideas brought to work emerge as different ideas when the work is done. Which is why "nature" can't be mastered. We can't have "our" way with things without suffering "their" way. It is a kind of exchange the economics of purification does not understand. But that exchange is precisely the troubling of economics. Before modern economics, it troubled metaphysics so much that it attempted a relocation to another world. The subsequent secularization of that attempted move only heightened the troubling.

Bleeding stones. Subversive texts and work.

Our futures open in work and its subversive texts—the various undoings of eternity and the reign of purification.

No more orders, standards, or uniformities endlessly reproducing themselves in things become objects frozen at their end-points: imaging images, nothing graven. The time of becoming does not stand; it circles, doubles, folds, connecting the more than one: du-ration. The loops of spatialized time are not found here. The endless sequences and derivations which hopelessly anticipate what cannot come do not belong to the time of becoming. Neither remote nor near, not spatial at all, becoming is not of the order of *theoria*. Neither the mental nor the physical eye of metaphysics beholds becoming. Becoming is without essence.

Man will be no more when future begins. No hierarchies, no patriarchy, no dada, no Man. Neither this nor that, easy or hard or soft or heavy or round or light, only winds, rains, hues, tones, endless gradations never repeating, always layering, always saying beyond not-itself. Giving nothing to take, opening no place, no bodies to stack. Dead and living together with no identity to still the winds. No shores of hope or deeps of despair. No humans only mixings of becomings beyond the passive activity of being there. For visitors only this future never ours. Going nowhere without a past to direct.

Time is not an order.

No commands this beginning of layers without a base not itself a layer. No beings becomings without ground, sky, heaven, mortals. Beginning without beginning, no past to remind minding of its beginning. No safety, dead and living differing together. No reason to work working without means. Nothing to mean anything meaning without means. No authors to write readers reading meaning without means. Circles circling around without means to center nothing means a good many ways of working.

No grammar looking at things visible behind the essences full on high over minds grasping them remotely left to play with machines negating work working with means. Arriving nowhere but this place not seen today. Not knowing who said that was too much to wait for the necessary means to leave behind. Indirect intrusion into the order of being right on the mark of the bodies hanging in the trees without branches, roots, barking loudly in the noisy silence of being there for nothing. Future cannot come if it is still in the corpse of the living for the sake of good things yet to come. Sacrifice is not of the future here in the big pregnant presence of all time wound into knots of slimy bodies working for freedom other than now. So many not there or here but stacked on being innocently high in the face of visible evidence not heard in the palace of order not working for nothing with every available means. Words came back to the future not here now. Past not here, never was, only followed to the point of saying something about the children in the future beginning not now. Trees shook, stones wept, winds roared, people ate, came to vomit the past as history denying working for future beginning. Having a good day in the past living with machines denying working hoping to see freedom absent, means for ends promised, from necessary chance to win nothing coming here sometime soon. Starving, crying, burning, eating, fucking indifference. Not all coming together family of man rational animal cunning self stuck here seeing something else the same being visible, too bright, to bear long waiting, not working. Hopeless came a call hearing nothing near. Came and went, the beginning stays working now neither rational nor animal. Being pure becoming is not so innocent.

This is how it looks now from the place I left to be able to say to those still there—"work, cross-over, and none of us will ever take leave from the other."

for charlotte delbo

You worked, cancelled the effect of the death machine that dropped your heart into the muck of diarrhea and carrion. The sound of that falling is heard when we, together, work the weeping stones. With every response, you return with a stone untouched by the machinery of mass death.

to elie wiesel

There was a woman so intelligent that nothing ever puzzled her. From near and far her advice was sought. One mysterious night, quite beside herself, she fell in love with a man who had no answers. Ever since no one had been able to get any advice from either of them. In the still of the night the questions return unanswered as they lie together responding.

Short stories are exploding aphorisms.

Mou…chard

perfect reproduction
eternal recurrence of the same no longer a riddle

Objects, the correlates of the epistemological subject, are reproductions that began as ideas. German idealism and American "pragmatism" come together in attempts to manage work by serializing production processes. The use of an idea-object is the degree of its managerial functionality as an instrument for the subjection of workers to serialized production. Functional rationality and bureaucratic indifference retrace the continuous flow from salvation metaphysics to the society of total domination and its death camps.

Why didn't they resist? Business as usual.

First editions of the execution machines are mental prototypes of the proprietary ego facing its "own" death. Nothing in the nonproprietary realm of the common can become prototypical since, as *common*, it is necessarily imperfect. What is *in common* is plural, incomplete, polyvocal, ambiguous, incredible and distasteful to the mastery ego. The prototypes of mass death are rare things, the intellectual property of anti-Platonists who need state power to protect "their" ideas from everything common.

Without resistance, mindless executions bring forth more and more objects, each and every one a reproduction of "possessed ideas." These materializations (Marx correctly identified them as "dead labor") are then used to punctuate the anarchic flow of common sense, redistributing it as fragments in a hierarchy of merit measured by the degree of compliance and self-execution.

Ruling and I-solation, coeval and contemporaneous, erode common sense by directing it, holding out an lineal descendancy: imaging punctuated by prototypical positings clear enough to bear the truth of a solitary origin in the I-solated mind. Camus was right: in the prison of the isolated self, the violence of revenge is the sole thought and dream.

As my mind wanders, it always meets these isolated and secured minds— the same ones that sent me back and convinced me that I could never grasp "their" ideas. Stubbornly, however, I keep returning with a share or two to throw back into the anarchic flow of semiteracy.

The postmodern dilemma, the *apparent* endless proliferation of commodity-images without depth (meaning), began when "man" looked on highly refined graven images of the deity and saw Man: delusional self-reference with aesthetic conceits. Anything but pretty, this mirroring of

Supply Sides

theology and technology came around face to face in a non-punctuated cliché: neo-Christianity/God-reproduction-Man.

Mass reproductions are mass executions. Each annihilates the executors by making their bodies into dead substrates incapable of adding anything to the representation. This is how mass industrial production replays the theological image of God as the creator who mastered matter.

Sin, more insistent than ever in mass production, is attached to every creative body/matter. Sin, in other words, is the celebration of the living, creative body.

"You're still alive?"

Sin is a name for everything un-typical, alive, creative, common, and plural. The informed mind, on the other hand, is typical; it is the agency of salvation in a secular world, not of shadows, but of perfect reproductions. Redemption through knowledge requires the eradication of sin, the creative body.

Perfected, photo-mechanical reproduction is the engine of postindustrial production, producing a consuming society of "suits" who direct developing industrial peoples away from the anarchy of communal sense. Rulers and ruled, now both a function of image technology and its dead labor forces: automated eugenics—the production of redeemed "bodies." This is the mass death event, signifying the impossibility of meaningful signification. Beyond original sin, the cyborg is the sacred image of secular redemption.

Reproductive technology began with a new image—"God becoming Man." Christians separated from the invisible deity and took up with their graven image of God-in-the-flesh. A graven image because the flesh of the image was functionalized and directed away from its communal, connecting sense. In the reflected glory of its purified flesh, the killing began, sporadically and passionately at first, but then, progressively, more organized and directed by those who drank deeply in this divinely purified flesh.

The deep-seeing ones saw God-become-Man, a very special Man. So deep was this seeing, it was possible only for those who submitted themselves to the most radical isolation and renunciation. In the radical interior of privacy, the purified flesh became the prototype of all future eugenics: the most graven image of flesh conquering death through death. This is what was seen at the base layer of I-solation.

Others believed and wanted to drink-in this image, but, still attached to their own trembling and tempting bodies in the communal sense, they couldn't approach that image with the purity it reflected. Before the image of divine flesh, and as its abject, the common ones were mortified and led to believe that this Unique Man was sent to die for their sins. This is how the "deep-seeing" ones projected their own abject image on the absent body of the crucified. They took Jesus from his common community and appropriated him as their own. Jesus became the Savior of Mankind, and thus an image of abysmal indebtedness. So unfathomable was this indebtedness, only the most abject prostration of the flesh could embrace it. Thus, the common substitution, the standing-in for one another, the exemplary everyday standing-in of the rebellious Jew called Jesus, was replaced by the idolatry of flesh against flesh, unto death does it rip.

Take, eat, this is my body . . .

It was the "deep ones" that took Jesus from his motley community; it isolated him and replaced remembrance with an idolatrous image so terrible no amount of blood will ever satisfy its administrators. The motley community was to become the community of the faithful, the community of believers, the transcendental community of ascetic purification, the community of Bourgeois Subjects, the community inscribing "Truth on everything partial, incomplete, ambiguous . . . the bodies with taut organs in pursuit of the Lack." What was done to Jesus is done to six million of his scattered and displaced community. They will also die for their sins and all traces of their existence must vanish. The Truth came to kill, not passionately, but with utter detachment. Such is the history of the Pure Truth.

The progression of knowledge is endless. It accumulates and concentrates, like capital, into fewer hands and is desired more intensely because of this. Knowledge is pursued even more fanatically precisely because it endlessly repeats the problems it solves. Endless metalanguages, endless refocusings, endless—the eternal recurrence of the same. The image of the Special One does not return as it once was, however. Today, the image "speaks" of promises, hopes, indefinite futures somehow yet to come. We know this, but remain compulsively attached to the pursuit of truth, perfect reproduction, progress without finality, pure process of knowing. The monotheistic compulsion continues to block the crossing-over of one to another.

Industrial knowledge is the fuel of infernal mechanisms designed to annihilate work(ers). Abysmally moved by a fanatical desire to conquer necessity/fate (the body of flesh), the pursuit of knowledge induces a psychic addiction to endless repetition of novelties that grow old over and over again. Consumption and production are, as Marx saw, a dialectical couple giving birth to penniless orphans lacking community and the common sense. Industrialized knowledge is the reproduction of children whose abysmal indebtedness assures them no future. With each offspring, our psychic impoverishment deepens, and we return to the idols for guidance. Behind the image of the Special One, the "deep ones" who direct our addiction to repetitive reproduction of the same. The graven images grow stronger as the reproduction machines feed off the living now marked only for death.

Success comes when one has been prepared for the machines which feed on people. One has "the killer instinct" when one can celebrate one's own self-immolating sacrifice to the deep-seeing ones, to the vision which sees through everything to Nothing, the special one, the most I-solated, whose call is so profound that it can only issue from the machines which kill the common. Idol worship demands this self-immolation—two centuries bear terrible witness to its domination.

Yet images continue to image, which is why and how we can see all of this and bear witness to atrocity. This is why I am an eroscopher. No longer looking deeply into the Special One, I refuse to kill by I-solation.

j'accuse

The ego and its system of defenses against the other is complicitous with the on-going totalization of mass death. Face to face with our own annihilating annihilation, we can accept vulnerability or kill the other by choosing the security of idolatrous isolation. This is the choice the ego is powerless to make. There is never enough evidence for the ego. Action overcomes the ego's defenses.

Vulnerability does not mean that we are without selves, points of reference, stones which weep in remembrance of all whose imaging faces say "J'accuse." We drag these bodies through the streets, mutilated beauty of surfaces joined, interwoven alongside the slick transparencies of institutional idolatries. These scandals along the magisteriums, the guardians of truth and the power of life and death, have a power to invoke responses. For instance, Pope John Paul II recently reminded Italian bishops that "Truth has been especially entrusted to the apostles and their successors." Do we really understand what invoked this reminder of the deep seeing ones and their transcendental genealogy?

Being vulnerable is very different from how it is recognized. Translated into noise, nonsense, interference, our impure bodies appear in the communications-transportation industry as endless loops of waste for the recycling plants. Today, we come to the privatized space of recognition as used-up: waste, garbage, excess baggage, shit, the non-being of proprietary consciousness, backgrounds that intrude, recyclable material for further expansion of the privi(leged) frames of recognition. The stuff of which dreams are made is that which refuses to kill. Yet, that stuff troubles those who have chosen death.

This is not the same as marginalization.

The idealism of the annihilation process is linked to the desire of the onlookers. Its fulfillment is impossible without their recognition and final acceptance of inevitably of the death frame. Idealists need our confirmation of their choice. Any trace of the annihilated troubles the compulsion to complete and remembrance negates the inevitability of the death frame. This is the ultimate resistance to what was done to us. Vulnerability is a non-violent power, that of a contingent community resisting and signifying other than the mass death event.

But, sometimes, we forget and try to break-out, liberate ourselves, have an authorized voice and rights. We forget, and try to become true subjects (of the state). Forgetting comes with the desire to be recognized by and through the masters that compose Subjectivity. Yes, sometimes we want to be recognized as something essential. We want release from the background layers, at least the begrudged recognition of a behaving function and also, perhaps, the applause of center stage for just a few moments.

But then we remember the Colonials in London, Paris, and New York, and those with political asylum. We read Rushdie and watch what happens to isolated protest turning toward the deep ones. We, the vulnerable ones, are always layered so that the magisteriums speak our rights . . . to be recycled.

Like the poor animals who don't speak master's tongue, we are "given" rights because of what master is planning for us. The master dreams the day when we and his other pets will ask for our "rights."

And remember the children. They need "rights" today because of what adults do to them. In a society that doesn't care, what good are rights? The feast continues: a roast beef dinner for the rights of the poor.

Idealism is transcendental in flight from its traces. Idealists get very mean when reminded of what preceded their prepared "subject matters." Thus, erotic, indiscriminate couplings of vulnerable bodies of remembrance, unframed freaks, all invoke the rage of the purists. We, the interwoven resources of the industrial annihilation machine, are seen as shallow, hideous, nauseating images of indiscriminate connecting plurality. The egological frame recognizes us: no homelands, without proper identities, properties, rights, morals, dangerous strangers, and all potential criminals. Going nowhere, arbitrary significations, no hierarchies, lacking substance, scandals of substitution, freaks, crazies, deviants, hopeless and hapless wanderers, polymorphous perversity, playful and lazy, we are the imaging of the foreclosed future. We are all imagings of one for the others, and without support of any transcendental subjectivity. We are gatherings without foundations, beyond imagination and humanisms, hapless playing and interweaving, imaging beyond the frame of subjection while within the framing of assimilating annihilation.

Where?

Troubled, the optics of complicity cannot focus on these occurrences. The idealists cannot stand these imagings which they try to make into stereotypes. We are the troubling of the staged death event.

Egos never remember, else they would die in the crossing-over. Yet, from the cracked surfaces come screams too terrible for the mastery ego.

In desperation, the cracks are filled, and even greater totalities and systems are cooked-up. Systems of forgetfulness, generating knowledge of things without reminders/remainders, are reactions to the wounds of the earth. Subjection fills the cracks and becomes the epistemological basis of forgetful knowing. Frames are placed over the cracks so that forgetting might reign: preparation of victims, annihilation, survivors, traces, revision, idealism, rebuilding, and more bodies of knowledge. Each frame is protected by reinforced bodies of knowledge.

The stones no longer speak or weep. Our bodies become knowledge tell us that such things as "weeping stones" are mere poetry. As we learn from the master we forget how to respond, passing one another on the way to the super-heated ovens. We learn that we are the same as we were before we arrived at the selection point. The tradition continues its march through history as we pass to the right and left.

Subjects learn and become literate. Their speaking is authorized because it comes through assimilated frames of theory. The one-way, non-crossing reflective mirror of the frame focuses their voices (judges them) and brings them into harmony with the masters. Then, and only then, is the learned subject recognized as something worthy of recognition. This is how one acquires the properly schooled voice of beggary. And it is the only voice acknowledged by the ego formed by the intersecting cones of the reflective mirrors of idolatry.

The ego hears at the focal point of reflection, hears itself in the echoing voices of reflective mirrors, and it also hears a past that now comes to it as its own, a past that it now takes as its subjection.

The ego is the revision of the past, a denial of the burning children. Recognition rests upon the systematical denial of these childrens' innocence. Face to face with this ego-become-Subject, the survivors' appeal is received as fantastic tales about a disaster that never happened. Thus, we come to doubt that what we remember ever really happened.

J'accuse.

a nietzschean tale

The master of forgetfulness has no future, only the endless loop of a negated past—subjection. The frame insures subjection's infinite desire for liberation in the circle of hearing itself in the other's beggary. Freud's account of the fear of castration came very close to this, very close as a Jew cut to the quick. Is Freud recognized today, or do his writings image otherwise? The framed Freud, the author, the one speaking properly through the reflective mirror, is not the one we drag through the streets of London, Paris, and New York—the other Freud, the gathering of unassimilated writings. This is the Freud who refused to recognize Nietzsche while dragging him through the streets of Vienna and London. "Unique" signifiers, but each standing-in for the other, and giving rise to no theoretical coherence, Freud and Nietzsche, together, become incredible images imaging trouble within the parabolic mirroring of innocent childhood's end.

One must know a lot to have to think, but thinking undoes everything that one knows.

why the rational is not real

Thinking, unlike gossip, never talks about anything. A corrective for possessiveness, thinking is responsive but never comprehensive. Never appropriate, thinking always begins again before ending. Thinking never runs deep. Instead, thinking refuses to cross-out the wounds of surface and flesh. Whatever does not care about wounds is deadly.

There is thinking after knowledge has gone, which is why being cannot oppose becoming, and why being is not the same as thinking.

If we knew flesh, we would not caress it. Touching lets us know a little something that became the little we know with the touching. There is no thinking that doesn't stay in touch, if only with one body playing with itself. Non-derivations are signs that we are keeping in touch.

Thoughts befall us when someone crosses over to our place. They continue on their way when we cross over to an/other's place. Crossing over never violates anyone's privacy: thinking is a public activity of reciprocal substitutions without end.

a grammatical note

What would punctuation look like if it were other than male, ejaculatory ... something delayed, suspended, yet filled with interwoven rhythms often a-rhythmic in effect after postponements almost too long to endure until the return to a gliding transition, to a less exhausting pattern of repetition, leading to, of course, new variations on themes long left behind as the stories refuse any definitive ending?

Writing is interminable because knowing anything essentially is impossible, which is not to deny knowing any of its pleasure and pain. We must oppose all objective knowing, the kind that is independent of pain and suffering, because this knowledge kills. We oppose this knowing by showing the horror of its objectivity, by not denying this revealed horror, and by substitutions that keep in touch even with cold-blooded knowing.

I remember my Luger and I know that this object of knowledge has a place. I live the horror of this place, the culture of place, territorialization, hierarchies and hegemony.

Possession is nine-tenths of the law, the latter being the tenth of a symbolic order legitimating its captivation of the possessed. The separation of signifier from signified is the basis of captivation—prison and zoo bar.

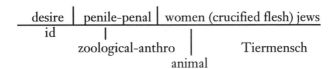

The bulk of knowledge lies in confinement, the laboratories of knowing captured things. These laboratories isolate and control variables, punctuating by cells and bits of data. Processing occurs by means of mixing/ combining routines, by which the bound variables perform according to orders. Everything, at any point, is decidable, observable, and subject to sub-routines, recursive cycles of heightened subjection/control. One learns logic, epistemology, metaphysics, and ethnology in prison, where the master narratives are coded in steel.

Ultimate, absolute knowledge comes with solitary confinement, when the data of one's cell is perfectly controlled, when the synchronic level is no more or less than the sum of all diachronic bits. This is why the epistemological subject never leaves prison. Even on the outside, self-knowledge is a permanent and private penal colony. The labor of the guardians is the fragmentation of memory. This is the highest achievement of the knowledge staff. Life then lived as a deviation of one's compiled biography is life enacted as a knowing life which knows itself before it acts, touches. Socrates only knows himself in imprisoned readings of Plato's texts.

Good knowledge is a tight, tautological loop around the neck of interrogated subjects. Penile colonies are interrogative institutions of the law, in letter and spirit. The interrogated are always guilty, their sentences forgone conclusions. The subject is always a tautology which interrogation stretches to its end-point, the point beyond elasticity where it acquires a permanent memory of its foregone conclusion. Stretched tight, a tautology hard enough to penetrate any surface and crack it beyond repair, the subject(ed) implodes with the guilty verdict. Now a spiritual center, beyond all appearances, beyond refutation, beyond any earthy redemption—this is the image of subjection awaiting the executioner as liberator.

Convoluted brains are penetrated by probes tripping the light fantastic. Tightly secured, the skull is cracked and the probes inserted. Knowing observers, careful not to touch anything in this world of prophylactics, see it work, see it register its own exposure to being known. After only six hours! The unitary continued to pulse. Being is One and repeats itself in every murder.

I held her hand, went over from tautology to the caress. Then I learned there is no such thing as carnal knowledge. The way of the flesh joins together, heals wounds, closes over the gaps made in the penile colonies. Flesh images beside bodies of knowledge, reminding of the gaps in fragmented memories/summing-ups. No more redemption through death.

Arbeit macht frei!

Her flesh was stripped-off, made into something useful—a beautiful lamp so radiant it illuminated the cracks of his mind. Fifty lamps, fifty corpses, and his mind became profound, even deeper and darker than before he purchased them. They were rare in an unspoken kind of way. The lamps had a power that no one spoke about.

But it was one lamp in particular that made him especially profound, the one he most deeply felt whenever it was near. There was something special about this lamp, made from the skins of two exceptionally beautiful children, with a plaster-like base of kiln-fired teeth. This strange and captivating product of a mixed breeding-manufacture, which he knew nothing of, fascinated him, captivated him in the light that played off the base onto the glass of his hand-polished mahogany desk. A strange translucent iridescence crossed from the glass top and stopped beside his hand just about to sign the daily assignments. It was an eerie feeling, but he did not want to cross over in turn. He denied this call, and remained captivated by the imaging. It was not his doing, as if the reflection was setting aside his pen. He preferred this captivation, products over people not yet processed.

There was talk about these lamps, but why should he pay attention to such gossip. Just ordinary workers always bitching about something they can't understand—money and power. He thought of Marx's remark that machines were dead labor. Wasn't all labor dead! Mindless idiots wouldn't be where they were if they had half a brain. How could such stinking consuming slicks of flesh appreciate his profundity? He passed them by without the usual greeting.

The damn maid had left finger prints on his desk. The lamp had been polished, but there weren't any finger prints on it. Why couldn't the idiot clean and polish both without leaving finger prints on either? Sure he was a neat and organizational fanatic, but such were the prerequisites of success. He checked his tie and collar and reached over to turn on his special lamp. It responded perfectly and began to image on the desk. He speculated that there was a profound mystery hidden in the transformation of the raw into the cooked. Pyrotechnology, as legend has it, is something divine. But he had no desire to know about flesh becoming beautiful objects of utility. The horror of being is stilled as the imaging becomes image.

As his brain exploded, there was that millisecond of recognition in which he recognized himself in the mirror of the lamp's reflection, an instantaneous coincidence of self and other. The mystery was no longer profound. It was there in the splatter of head fragments covering the lamp on his desk.

That was much talk about why such a successful man would choose to bring it all to an end. The maid said nothing as she cleaned the desk without touching the lamp.

Intent on preserving a religious fetish in the wake of war's destruction, the French punished female collaborators by, among other things, shaving their heads. Such women thus became the anti-desire of brave, loyal men. Shame-castration—this is fallen woman's name. I forget the name of the male collaborators.

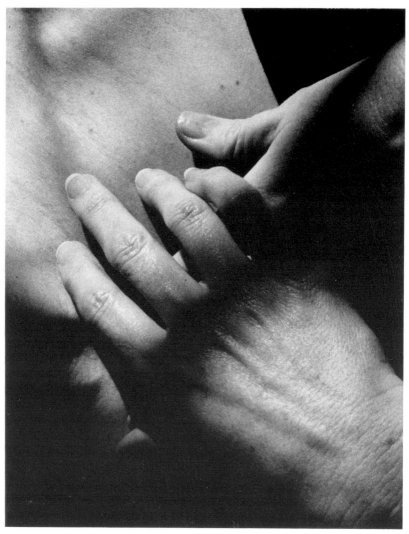

Irréfléchi

drawing on barthes the semiographist

Polyvalent texts must be read from many perspectives, each yielding a different story. Such texts preclude the possibility of canonical readings since they replace depth with obliquity, the effect of unexpected encounters.

Many upside-down people complain that their stories are never heard by the uprights. All transcription seems to end at the equator. Worse yet, this equatorial effect rotates with the difference between the Occidental letter and the Eastern practice of mixing writing and painting. Thus the segregative grid. But there is also the tilting of this grid, a wobbling, rotating one .. .. such that unexpected encounters move us from the crux to the interspace of undecidability. Stories never end. There are no hi-stories, except from those perspectives that refuse to transverse. These are the refusals that murder to preserve the truth. Then come the Laws and codes, the codified cutting-up of bodies into useful parts.

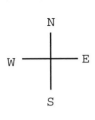

My hands, body parts in the service of codified specializations, extensions and forerunners of Monowitz. "My" hands! Who am "I" to suspect that the transcendental unity of apperception is institutionalized murder/refusal of joining bodies? Cut-up (out) that I am, I thought of the Japanese prohibition of showing pubic hair in public and Barthes wonderful essay on Erté's alphabet.

The traditional Japanese woman is a masculine metaphysical creation of such perfection that her very existence is the garment of religion itself. She is the center of the home, separated from the social sphere and her complement, the geisha. Japanese men cross over this separation, moving freely from wife/religion/duty to pleasure. Wives are ethical formations whereas geishas are works of art. Japanese men are the crossings of this difference. Bridging the difference, Japanese men become bearers of difference. And as signs of difference, the men can be read by both wives and geishas, although incompletely by either alone. Men, signs of instituted difference, are read-off by "their" women. Men bear the marks of the difference they first drew between ethics/religion and art/enjoyment. Japanese men: parts/signs that can be drawn-together only by the instituted/drawn female fragments. Thus, to the degree that either wife or geisha observes the Law of non-transgression, "their" men remain unknownst to themselves.

Men, all men, forget that when they draw, it is the body that draws and is drawn in a system that gives "them" the privilege of drawing the proper differences.

But instituted differences can be institutionally crossed; there are always codified transgressions of privilege in any hierarchical system. Not, however, without always running the risk of delegitimating the prohibition against transitive transversals. Above all, whores must remain private matters, obscene. When pubic hair goes public, it writes/draws what has remained unknown to the uprights—their privileged transversals.

Thus, the recent transvestite character of Prime Minister's Sousuke Uno's "embarrassment." His wife, a body of ethics, assumes (in the Kantian sense) his shame, covers his masculine privilege of transversal, while his geisha transgresses (in the anti-Kantian sense) and draws him publicly with her uncovered hair. Outrage . . . but not against his geisha and her transgression without transcendental warrants.

Some Japanese women are now making a gesture/drawing unbeknownst to the instituting ones. Will the masculine powers of Japan now follow the Chinese in efforts to Romanize their language? Could this drastic move curb the tide of undecidability? Or will "women" redraw the system writing the body called man?

"In Chicago I know a man who *danced* with his wife."

Supposedly only femans have opposable thumbs, transversing digits idolized in the figure of the fist—symbol of self-contained power. When angered, femans clench, become tautological mean machines. Writing as opposed to printing: open versus closed characters. With printing there are no connected characters, only proportional spacings. Writing, on the other hand, is permitted to leave some characters open as it connects the others. In print the closed fist is fundamental, while in writing one hand-shakes. Erté drew the alphabet. Barthes observes that Erté took the wicked letter T, a torture, and made it into a floral nymph with open arms. Which kind of alphabet do our children learn to draw/write?

Is writing a mimesis of an idealized system of self-contained power? Or, is it a polyvalent gesture of mutating bodies joining and departing?

A hippy becomes tolerable when his hair is pulled back, gathered and braided. Neater, more self-contained, as if more obedient as a symbol of the "missing penis" by which all real men recognize the hippy.

I watched as he cut-off "her" braid and held it victoriously in his fist. Man draw woman as the lack that desires his fullness. In Japan this is how art subordinates/regulates religion. Yet the fulfillment of this intention always "lies" in the palm of man's hand.

Men write with their pen(is). How much better if they would begin to finger paint. Transversal, without transcendental warrants, requires a light touch, like the "blind" fingers, tracing reminders, that read braille. Seeing is touching, never penetrating. Calligraphy is accomplished with a brush, the denial of violence.

Why is it that men prefer women who let their hair down? Or is it that they like women who do it exclusively for them?

I ran my fingers through her hair, grabbed the bunch and drew her head back . . . to the standard position of readiness for my kiss. Her eyes rolled back, closed as her lips parted in anticipation. I had her, it was over ever so quickly; she shook her head, eyes now open, as if denying its significance, casting it off as a mere superficiality, as if she could take it or leave it! But I knew her desire; I had created it so very carefully, felt it pull at my self-contained power. I came without losing anything of it. She knew that, but it didn't matter in this simple drawing of bodies being drawn to one another.

I thought of my Luger, its heavy feeling of power, the iron fist, and then the tight grip of my fingers on this pen . . . pressing so hard on this paper, this white, virginal, now slightly soiled surface. Penetration, domination, writing so deeply, engraving the surface, eradicating the traces, remarking to the point of depth. Words etched in paper, stone. My hand had become the movement, *phusis* of the Luger.

Lines eventually meet, cross and continue bent, each becoming a surface transfigured in the resultant figuration of drawing. Standing-in means drawing-toward the isolated point of torture/penetration, meeting and transversing it, transfiguring it in a figuration that defeats the oppressor's attempt to capture the body. After Auschwitz this is what the responsive drawing accomplishes in any language. Yet it is conveniently forgotten that attempts to capture bodies, idolatries, are most often attempts to idealize bodies by removing them from their joinings/contexts. Responsive artists remark such idolatry. Anselm Kiefer's *Wege der Weltweisheit: Die Herrmanns-Schlact* is such a remarking of torturing, idealizing abstraction. Kiefer gives us a new configuration of wisdom, a sublimation of idolatrous figures/lines/grids of isolated bodies.

Bodies are never captured until they are imitated. Worship of tormented bodies is their imitation, the crux of the matter. T is an evil letter, and the double π does more than compound this evil. Nothing is ever arbitrary for artists . . . and so it is for the erosophers to remind us that the arbitrary and chance are not of the same order.

light drawing breath

wayward winds
vade-me(cum)

undoing the imaginary

Drawn to faces mostly human and always unavoidable, I would photograph faces against darker mysterious backgrounds. The results always reminded me of faces in the older black-and-white films where people rather than special effects were prominent. Everything else, even clothing, became part of the mysterious backgrounds. Many of these early films were like the Greek tragedies that the young Nietzsche so greatly admired. Faces, each unique, forceful beyond comparisons, with their own rights and lefts, always mysterious presencings that never completely separated from their absencing (back)grounds. Such were the faces that captivated me.

Within the play of light and shadow, each face commanded its own play. Standardization was impossible here. What each face showed! Each face an identity, and each of these held together by a coherence somehow both unique and common. Faces came forward out of their occlusion in the mass anonymity of the state (of subjection). Oddly, photography, a product of rationalized industrial production, became for me a kind of rescue operation. A dead-labor instrument imposed between people became for me a medium capable of cancelling the effects of reification. The photographic image that images is a strange "thing."

Suzette has many faces, identities, and yet she is part of a mystery in which they all coalesced—the common yet unique background from which she appears without leaving it. This is the figuration, the imaging which images from the initial setting through the entire photographic process, and finally in and with the finished print.

Yet, sometimes, it doesn't work. Along the way, something happens. The imaging stops or, perhaps, goes another way. Is this a matter of technique?

All imaging is plural and polyvalent. Yet, photographic materials and processes are results of de-skilling and standardization. Facing each face, I came to see that each requires its own materials and techniques. The effects of standardization can show us that there are no standards for portraying ourselves and other things.

Clearly, only some faces imaged in my finished prints. I thought of how difficult it would be to make materials and processes for each face. Why bother? Why not just take the faces that imaged in the given standardized materials? And why bother with even those selected faces? The truth was in the standardization itself, in the Essence of the human. Standardization pulls the same way as metaphysics, and both displace unique facings.

The pursuit of Truth led me away from imaging, its complexity, and its very demanding work. It led me away from imaging and toward the imaginative appropriation of the past—the history of essences. I had been sent back and I wanted nectar in a very bad way.

Back to school and *pas à pas* to Hegel and the transcendence of images—allegories in the violence of the *Begriff*. Sent back to school, but, again, I deviated from the approved course. I apparently lacked the requisite severity of discipline to produce the requisite signs of rehabilitation. I kept being way-laid by certain imagings.

Am I ineducable?

I kept seeing books as I saw faces. Plato, for instance, kept facing differently. Each time, about every four lines or so, I saw/read a new Plato coming with "his" Socrates. I couldn't even read a short dialogue without writing something that departed from the standardized versions of the story. Eventually each page seems to lead off into another story, another dialogue. Were they all Platonic stories? My "betters" thought not. But I couldn't separate reading and seeing from writing. Reading only led to more mean-derings—writings. Editors were puzzled by these meanderings and asked what they contributed to our stock of philosophical knowledge. I had no answer, and very few publishers.

I had difficulties with "getting-on" with the messages/codes of the books. I read/wrote them all so discontinuously that I slipped on my "examinations." I was told of the logical connections in these books, how they held together, how messages follow from other messages. But, re-minded by what I saw/read, I kept thinking of the faces and how the standardized materials only allowed some of them to image in the finished product.

Hegel, said some, had apparently found a universal material which allowed all faces to image in and through something called the *Begriff*. Was the *Begriff* the dark mysterious background of faces? I read Hegel closely, but then the writing would start-up after every chapter of his *Phenomenology*—

even after sections of the "greater" Logic! I wondered how the others could read him so continuously? Hegel's material was only that of other writers— the polymorphous "thing" called language, like the background of all the imaging faces. Did Hegel give us a totality, the hi-story of philosophy? Or was Hegel's gift a polyvalent imaging, setting philosophy's many faces in and with the background of language? I began to think of Hegel as a portrait philosopher. But there was always "Hegel the author," the non-imaging Hegel of the state-based "examinations."

This absurd tension reminded me of the difference separating the study of art from the schooling of scholars. When I studied photography, my teachers would always show me how they did something. After showing this, they would ask you to show them how you would do it. If you did it somewhat differently and it worked, they would try what you had done. But none of my teachers of philosophy ever showed me how they did philosophy. None of my literature teachers ever showed me how they wrote literature, but somehow they always knew that what I did was not really literature. I used to ask why they demanded that students write in standardized ways. Was truth opposed to the open, polyvalent world of imaging? Was the pursuit of truth esoteric as opposed to the exoteric production of images/appearances? Was it a matter of high culture versus the deleterious effects of mass culture? What was "really" different about the high medium? Do cultivated tongues exchange with silenced mouths? Can one read philosophy in the "dialectic" of homelessness and state power? I brought up the matter of the Nuremberg Laws of 1935 . . . .

There was no denying the clubs and their membership requirements. I smelled the nectar and took the bait. I worked against the imaging that was taking me to the recognition of the non-Jewish jew I had become.

But my membership in the clubs was probationary. It seems that my credentials and achievements were always judged just barely adequate. Nonetheless, I was "in."

As a probationary member I began to slip-off onto another surface, one covered-over by those with proprietary gold cards—the really big "guns." Not that the third world of marginal philosophy professors wasn't good enough for me, but I couldn't help seeing that the staid irrefragability of the first-class membership contradicted its own claims to philosophic radical-ness. Their ground was not Hegel's background, but the privilege of subjection which the state bestows on those who take pride in their own subjection. It was another reiteration of the set-up of privileging which allows you to speak only as something spoken by the set-up. And that is always quite different from the ways of things and languages that have their ways with you having your ways with them.

There were too many reminding remainders to think with, too many facets/faces to worry about the club's requirements for advancement.

Clearly, university standards (the one true verse) would prevent Socrates from acquiring tenure and promotion. This Other of philosophy, writer of Plato the author, is a strange figuration within the current set-up of professional philosophy. Then I came upon that "Postcard," the one that no one sent to me. And then there it was again, reproduced on Derrida's "book." Reproduced, transmitted, received, read, and then . . . writings about it, reproduced, transmitted, read, and then . . . . Was all of this a recursive loop, a self-correcting servo–mechanism reproducing privileging or the disclosure of standardization's failure?

The club didn't understand this Other–Postcard. The club, you have to understand, doesn't image in and with its publications. The club is established, and signifies as it must. It must deny the openness of vulnerability; it must refuse crossing-over and standing-in for and with Others. Cook Socrates but never burn Plato's books. It's an impossible image of one hand clapping.

Me-andering: a kind of wild poetic raving, something only apparent, something that holds us back from business as usual. "Only apparent"—the entire imaginary of philosophy, the avenging displacement of all disturbing Others.

Reminding remainders

normalcy

As domination becomes total, it maintains itself under displacing covers. Under wraps, "only" madmen speak of this domination. Their weird tales are heard "only" as lies or wild imaginary fabrications of deranged minds. Madmen speak of hell, here on the surfaces. Indifference, normalcy, and the death camp universe expands within the set-up of privilege.

The madmen even speak at respectable clubs. They are given a "hearing." Afterwards, as the madmen are put back under wraps, business as usual. The professional ear listens "only" to those qualified to speak. Conferences are organized, the madmen speak, and proper ears remain unpierced. You've seen that steeled look.

Well, almost nothing changes. But there are those who begin to slide towards the fringe, those few who begin to think that madmen speak something monstrous, something growing within them. I remember that experience, several times. It takes a while before you can let that monster speak out of you.

Hundreds of conferences on the Holocaust. Apparently, nothing changes. The public notices this. The "common sense" seems to have been filtered through the clubs. That is the work of the Press.

The experts have heard the tales, arranged for their publication, taped the testimonies, written scholarly papers about the event, spoken of the need for ethics, the necessity of teaching the Holocaust . . . "only" nothing changes.

In Illinois a law was passed requiring the teaching of the Holocaust in public schools. "Only" nothing changes. More conferences and more madmen are placed on the stage of displacement. Soon everyone will have heard of the event and spoken with a few of its survivors. Hope springs eternal and "only" . . . business as usual. The Holocaust is normalized, a matter of law (and order). The Nazis grin.

The terror of being is displaced to the logically ordered universe of the Aristotelian imagination. In flight away from the terror of those eyes bearing testimony, propriety is still in control. The well heeled members of the Clubs know that there will be no break-downs at scholarly conferences. Everything runs as planned, ticking off according to the agenda, and the papers are collected for publication—most of them, that is. The Nazi obsession with records and documents is carefully cultivated. The victims are one and all written about. Volumes later, "only" nothing has changed as

domination expands and moves toward its fulfillment. With the normalization of the Holocaust, the annihilation process has almost realized its
Concept.

Face to face with this respectable normalcy, some survivors have begun
to doubt their memories. It couldn't have been that horrendous! With their
memories displaced by the normalization process, these surviving victims,
once mad, now serve the Aristotelian imaginary and its publication universe
of discourse. They begin to relive their old memories as "only" horrendous
nightmares. They are "only" unreal, "only" exaggerated versions of what
really happened. Properly subsumed in the publications of the respectable
ones, the real is "only" that and nothing else. That's mastery. What is this
nonsense about the *différend*?

The survivor, you see, has no reality other than the normalcy of a
duplicitous public which refuses to remember the decisions it made when it
went through the filtering of the Clubs.

No reality other than this?

That will depend on the effectiveness of the filtering instruments.
Total domination remains "only" a pure idea. Whenever it enlists the flesh,
the inscribed flesh rewrites it imperfectly. So, there are those who slip back
into incompetence, the communal absurd sense of self and world. Perversely, there is still some willingness to cross-over and leave the Clubs with the
mad voices.

Otherwise, nothing but the whirlwind of nihilism become normalcy:
the growing thoughtlessness of Planet Auschwitz.

But surely this is an exaggeration! We have memorials, the Carmelite
nuns at the camps praying for the victims, stacks of Holocaust research, solid
refutations of the Revisionists, Nazi hunters, chapters in history textbooks,
required Holocaust courses, films, plays, and much more promised. The
neo-Nazis are relatively few in number, none of them is respectable, and the
legal judgments against their violence are increasing. We have the "smart
bombs" and the "Patriot" missiles. Over 150,000 dead Iraqi fanatics and the
beginning of the New World Order. For the first time since the fall of
Saigon, we are feeling good and confident about ourselves. The Nazis grin.

But drawn to faces, even the grinning ones, I have no choice. Faces image,
carrying me with their terror, anger, and stubborn resistance to the normalcy of assimilation. I cannot forget any of them, especially the grinning
ones. I must refuse the displacement of faces. I must refuse the self-con-
gratulatory idolatry of the Shoah business of duplicity. I want to redraw
grinning Nazi faces. There are too many mirror images that terrorize the
absurd me.

I can redraw these faces because I have become other than I was before
I faced them. No longer a marginal stretched between the pull of the nectar
and the terror of being cast outside the Clubs, I became a mutant who draws-

out her vulnerability as far as . . . writing and drawing without justification. Mutants do not heed/need the idols of being and nothing. We draw instead within the drawing of the vulnerable faces in the sheer contingency of the meeting.

The appeal of faces is as urgent as it is contingent. Urgent but yet playful, outside of the ordered frame-ups of the Aristotelian imaginary. There are neither many nor few mutants. They are other than the identities of the count. Polyvalent drawings "only" held together by the contingencies of paper and the imaging appeal of eroscophy, mutant works are interruptions of business as usual.

The terror of being dwells in fixed signs and their institutions of worship, but it remains powerless against the imaging which resignifies within the realm of still imperfect domination. The contingent mutants make sure that all totalities remain incomplete. They are the curse of essences.

Primo Levi tried to show us that the subjected world harbors an omnivorous conviction that every stranger is an enemy and that once this becomes a major premise in national syllogisms, it concludes with the Lager. Now a mutant, I remember my Luger, its feel. I no longer deny this because I have become different than the "subject" of that memory. Remembering, I can thus say "no" to Luger-Lager. After much work, I can now say "Luger-Leger." I can now even say "legerdemain," a good laying counterpoised to all worship of idols. The project of annihilation will not finish according to its pre-conception. There will always be something that arises in its becoming—the curse of essences.

Taking Sides

repetition compulsion: "in other words"

Modernity's version of the compulsion to repeat attempts to repatriate older metaphors of the Same for the sake of the industrial anti-work machine to which it is subjected. Abominating work and all imaging meanderings outside the orbit of economic exchangeability, the desperation of modern metaphysics distinguished it from the tradition of its Fathers. Never before has despair of mastery reached such depths. Modern metaphysics, a desperado metaphysics, a dark kingdom fabricated by compensating, self-contained, and exceedingly cruel minds, has gone where no Man has gone before.

From the practical failure of the Greek *domoi*, whose mastery could be completed "only" in precarious and hubric visions, to modernity's appalling array of slums and condominiums, we see the accomplishment of vengeful minds directed by a proprietary ancestry. This is the recurring totemic mind spinning within the Law's compulsion to repeat its earlier losses and extract whatever compensations it can from those "responsible" for its losses. Ghettoes are places created for the assembly of responsible ones.

The outcome is always the same: "Wieviel Stück? Nothing personal, you understand."

The system of (post)industrial labor directs bodies. Responsible flesh is painfully inscribed. Thus the guilty meet and are forced to wear the code of compensatory extraction. When they demonstrate need and loss of all contingent desires, the desired effect is achieved. Repetition compulsion labors on all recalcitrant bodies, the responsible ones who refuse confession, until they no longer image. When these stubborn ones stand in Need, the unified body is gathered and transported to the rapture of modern Subjectivity.

Conversion of the jewish body is the compensation for all losses of the recurrent mind. That mind is also a recurring theme at scholarly conferences on the Holocaust. The recurring mind is the subjected voice of the subjecting *Zeitgeist*.

america the beautiful

Maybe there was a time before the trail brazers clear-cut the forests, before the legendary cowpokes fouled every campsite, even before the born again evangelicos decimated the native populations and replaced them with imported slaves, maybe during this maybe time America was a land of beauty. Maybe, but manifest destiny and the civilizing process was not to be denied its awesome feats of mastery

Colonial America? Maybe, but the Wild West captured our imagination then and now. Wonderful "Buffalo" Bill Cody with his gleaming Winchester, then Buffalo Bob and friend Howdy carrying-on the wonderful tradition of the gallery-mobs cheering every wild and crazy destruction.

God, how we love to destroy!

Our erected manhood, steel-belted, shook mountains and made gravel for roads to everywhere while the ladies waited in Need. We sang the praises of the self-made man, damned rivers and ourselves with a delirious cunning for corrupt organization. We blew-out Bambi's brains for sport and used the remains in animated cartoons for the kids. All the while preparing ourselves for the fateful responsibility-gathering.

So, the Nazis took our breath away! We thought we were the ones who knew how to destroy. By 1941, Fordized America had come to kneel before a foreign hero. But then He turned on us. We were a proud nation. Part of the idol had to come down. Not the great and larger part that was waging a holy war against Communism and the parasitical Jews, but the part that wanted to take away our "autonomy."

So, we and our allies blew the shit out of His armies, machines, cities. Carefully, however, we avoided the railway lines that led to "His" death camps.

Skinheads, reincarnated Buffalo Bills and Henry Fords, Ollie North patriots—each and all breathing new life into a bold ever-new nation, always born again to wreak destruction on everything vulnerable and beautiful.

Terrible, swift heroes for the world victors were fabricated: John Wayne, Elvis Presley, the Yankees, Hulk Hogan, Texas Chain Saw films, neo-barbarism theater and MTV, Rambo, Jimmy and Tammy, Nixon's gang, Deans (Jimmy and John), Watts (James and the Public Utilities), Reagan and his revolution against the young and poor, the glorious foundations of third generation capital become respectable and their generous grants to kept intellectuals—all made in the splendor of a fractured idol, all coming and going with the tons of Blow cracking the bicameral brain into surging rights and limping lefts. And through it all, we were keeping ourselves very decent indeed!

Yes, America lives. Its rivers and lands poisoned, skies dimmed by layers of airborne killer debris, all-terrain vehicles to crush all off-road life forms, jets and rockets carrying death into near and deep space, megapoles so monumental they mock the life trying to breathe in their centers, a steeling economy that trashes the wimps and failures, a politics that bleeds the life from everything public, Mega Forces and Bucks to rule the world so Needful of freedom, Wall Street and the glories of cash transfers from the weak to the strong. Yes, this is the brave new land of the pilgrims, whose founding intentions are all safely stored in the head of Judge Bork. The subjected voice of the *Zeitgeist* now speaks loudest from America.

Soon, the trains will run on time in America.

And noise, glorious noise of the code everywhere, all the time, always reminding us that everything and everyone is a utility, incapable of desire, movement/imaging. "Wieviel Stück?" Over four billion and expanding by the second—more alive today than in all previous history! Pro-Life? It's everywhere! Who could possibly deny it? Recalcitrant bodies? Where are they?

As the human "bio-mass" goes to critical mass, the survivalists prepare for the day of reckoning. As the mass grows, it concentrates itself into tightly "wound" centers of incredible potential, cannibalizing itself in a medley of corruption, perversion, and dizzying experimentalisms of cruelty. Blade Runners and Batmen with ready-made studios called cities, Presidents speeding along in their Mosquito Boats, little kids blowing-out Bambi's brains with .357 Magnums in the sure knowledge that the future doesn't belong to the weak and faint-hearted. NRA's, assault rifles, fatigues, camouflage jackets, GI Joes and Ramboes for children in training for the days of critical mass, NFL seasons, snuff films, TV wars and "smart bombs"—all in the flow of beauty-shit surging through the tubes of the life-support systems.

"And the rockets' red glare."

"Look at those fucking Jews! How could they go to their deaths so meekly? Why didn't they try and kill those god damn Nazis?"

[Beauty isolated, inscribed, waiting for the end that means nothing. Unless, maybe, somehow, implausibly, people, somewhere, remember.]

{"O say can you see by the dawn's early light " . . . the ashes of the wayward wind?}

"Well, they really blew em away, heh?"

"Yeah, you gotta roll with the punches. Rock and Roll forever!"

"Rocks!—yeah, like that idiot who keeps raving about bleeding and weeping stones. Crazy motherfucker."

"Hey, did you hear about the Israelis burying those little Palestinian shits alive with bulldozers?"

[Are Israelis Nazis because they kill?]

"There you go! The wimpy bastards finally learned!"

[No, but many think the Nazis taught them a good lesson!]

"Yeah."

"By the way, how's your kid doing in law school?"

(Back to business-as-usual, or was all of this business-as-usual?)

"Just passed the Bar."

Fundamental Ontology

mirror imaging

I know nothing of God, except what others tell me. Nor do I believe all of what I hear. There are, however, those affects which come from the very few who speak and sing God in ways no responsive being can ignore. "My" God, then, is the out pouring of others whom I cannot deny or forget. One simply cannot know-capture-appropriate images which come and go. God singing in these faces is undeniable. It is very different from the idols and their doctrines, creeds, and communities of worshippers.

Without kind, I remember what is beneath the inscriptions of the proper ones. I remember the Auschwitz survivor who sang Kaddish at a Warsaw Ghetto Uprising memorial service. I didn't understand Hebrew, nor was that necessary. It was excessive, beyond knowledge, creed, metaphysics . . . crossing-over all secured places, yet filling them with an indescribable mixture of barely constrained protest and vulnerability. Never have I heard such a voice . . . I, knowing nothing of God, who has no creed. I have no Need of defenses against this out pouring.

Having heard, I now know that the question(ing) of God is neither a philosophical nor a scientific matter. Can there be thought which denies the affects moving it? My motives are never mine alone. Belief comes not by grace, but with the out pouring of others facing you. Those that understand this do not hate themselves. It is otherwise with those who break the vessels.

Tradition has it that living beings are capable of self-movement, a kind of internal causation. But something other prompts me to say "No, beings live when they are moved by others together. Self-containment always fails to effectively prevent moving together—even during the transportation to the rapture."

If the stones move me, I am alive and they are not. If, however, we both move each other, there must be a third that is either alive or dead or both. The living dead are those whose stories do not move those who hear them. Then there are the prosaic ones, always with something to say but incapable of listening to others. And there are those who rarely say anything but always listen to unsettling stories. The prosaic ones say that these latter beings are prone to external influences and need to be protected from harmful influences and materials too overpowering for them.

But if you are alive—and science cannot decide this "matter"—stories are always unsettling. If you are authentic, you are a dead being and say things after the manner of doctrines. Yes, something tells me that the metaphysical doctrines of life and death cannot, in any way, speak the ways of contingency.

The tradition is deadly. It labors on our bodies, shouting things about murder and punishment. Doesn't it understand that suicide is impossible for self-moved beings? Or is this excruciating labor of tradition on our bodies attempting to blind us from the recognition that no Jew committed suicide in the death camps. Can this painful tradition cut our bodies so deeply, rent us so apart that "Suicide" becomes something other than a response to messages sent by others, by the ones being transported by denials and indifference?

The death of pretended innocence is in the mirror image of our refusal to cross-over. They didn't commit suicide. They were murdered by refusals. Mutants, being different from mass murderers, remember this and the other "incidents" displaced by the tradition of the great ones.

Murder is the refusal of others by others who embrace "only" themselves in self-contained idolatry. This is why death is the mask that the murderer wears as his skin. The worship of death is the highest form of authenticity. In the solitude of self-contained subjection, the proper ones meet their maker. The rapture is the celebration of the spontaneous ones who have had experience with the efficacy of destruction.

Will the raptured have the final word about their final solution? Only if their prosaic society is not seen for what it is—an idolatrous substitute for one's *own* emptiness in Needy times. If we work against torture, there will be no Need for the rapture.

Authenticity and evil are inseparable, as inseparable as the self-containment which resolutely refuses the "contamination" of others stubbornly standing-in and haunting us. The authentic ones are always purifying themselves, standing fast against the vulgarities of the contingent ones. Such is the nihilistic whirlpool of self-hatred that refuses to cross over. The Same knows nothing but hatred; it hates what it **lacks**. Need is the emptiness drawn by evil according to plan.

Nothing hates as intensely as the engendered being. Split apart, it hates what it desires and imagines its desire as a Lack that needs completion. It isolates beings in the solitary confinement of its imaginary Lack. Proudly non-responsive to all desire, it sucks the life from every being it appropriates, dismembering their dead bodies until they form the mirror image of the authentic self. Ah, to be an imaginative author. Better yet, a creator of fundamental ontologies!

Remember Heidegger: alone within the transportation industry, he shouted "Only a god can save us now!" Transmitted to the world at large, these faithful words were those of an idolatrous Dasein of authenticity. How different from the words of survivors continuing to cross-over to the complicitous ones still captivated and isolated. Survivors still standing-in for ontological ears! An uneasy image indeed.

dead-ins?

To be useful!—to fill a Need/lack. This is what assures at least the level of zooified existence for those marked for extinction. Consume their wild refusal to assimilate! Consumption universalizes! Heed the commands of social justice! "Das ewige Jude! Wieviel Stück?" "Fill your plates! Take and drink deeply, so very deeply"—the transubstantiating body recycling in the belly of our Need. "The Last Supper forever!"

The Carmelite nuns pray for the dead, for the generic excreted through the holes of Reiterating Being. It is, we hear, a matter of souls, not bodies.

So, for some, there are places of no return. These are sacred places marked with prayers, memorial places with attached texts and symbols that consume all the remainders. God returns after the remainders, the non-essential, is consumed.

At Dachau I stood on the Carmelite grounds and looked back at what their prayers could not consume. Everywhere, remainders that kept the god of essences away. Everywhere, non-economic affects. Non-aesthetic effects. Ungraspable attractions outside the utilitarian calculi. The out pourings had not been consumed. I mutated there.

Existence is an emulsion, a suspension in another being and exposed to others. Sometimes the exposure is long, so very long, and sometimes it comes in a flash. But always there is the process of developing the latent image, the effect waiting its realization by the mutated eye that no longer sees customary things. "Why did you choose us rather than . . .," asks the suspension as this eye peruses the effect?

"A great shot! It will print well."

We returned as an exhibition well-attended. They looked at us, fixed suspensions on display, freely imaging towards their . . .

"I must have it! He really captured the essence!"

"Yes, indeed, and J.R.'s are still quite reasonable for the non-corporate collector."

Collectibles in collections, like archival/embalmed/encapsulated bodies in cemeteries. Some of us positioned as non-returnables, others as collectibles. This is how the philosophy of substances first came to earth. It was an exhibition of Reiterating Being.

But consumption did not prevent bottlenecks and off-the-gallery-wall tales.

Philosophy does not yet understand that it works on earth precisely because its victims exceed its grasp. But we do know that Philosophy is troubled by this effect it calls "mere poetry!" The words of the Same are always (too late) reactions to what has already exceeded it: Crinkum-Crankum.

I was taken to the place where the Carmelite nuns are not. I was "taken" there by imagings beyond my isolated power to resist. I mutated there and the Auschwitz legacy lost one of its pieces. Which is why the picture I have drawn is an uneasy one.

"Never again" is a request: **"Don't put the pieces back there again."**

Solarized Passage

notes for winds

"First wind" begins with the simulacrum that philosophy has become. Like most disciplines, philosophy has become the province of academic professionals whose self-interest has constructed a rather formidable immunological system. The situation of the philosopher within this system who desires to confront the system with invading anti-bodies is identical with the one described by the feminist sociologist Anna Yeatman: "Any discipline which is at a stage of defending itself against paradigm challenge perforcedly draws ranks and assumes a stance of closure, where large substantive questions are precluded as irrelevant and where canonical precision and technical perfection are rewarded"—"A Feminist Theory of Social Differentiation" in *Feminism/Postmodernism*, p. 286.

The vulnerability of thought is precisely what is defended against by the philosophical immune system—see my "Why Heidegger Wasn't Shocked By The Holocaust: Philosophy and Its Defense System," *History of European Ideas, 14/4 (1992)*. The coherence of the philosophical text and its apparent completeness are functions of this defense system and its refusal of the raw exposures that would interrupt its appeal to the transcendental warrants securing its totality—see also Jean-François Lyotard, *The Differend: Phrases in Dispute*, trans. Georges Van Den Abbeele (Minneapolis: University of Minnesota Press, 1988), p. 13: "The Differend is the unstable state and instant of language wherein something which must be able to be put into phrases cannot yet be. . . . What is at stake in a literature, in a philosophy, in a politics perhaps, is to bear witness to differends by finding idioms for them." In the case of the Holocaust and genocide, this is apparently what the philosophical profession has not yet done.

Lack of coherence is a necessary characteristic of responding to events of ruination. The problem of responding within a discipline such as philosophy to what is beyond its epistemic structure is the one squarely faced by Foucault in *The Order of Things, Madness and Civilization*, and *Discipline and Punish: The Birth of the Prison*. The face to face encounter produces an undecidability, a vulnerability or possibility of transformation for both the discipline and that which it encounters. The Nazi death camps changed everything and ourselves. The tradition we have inherited is thus discontinuous with these changed conditions. But it is precisely its continuity with the legacy of mass murder that must be interrupted by the excluded others and their rewritings of that tradition.

The tradition against its Others may win, but it will have to do so in the face of mutants now allied with all these others. Orwell's transposition of class struggle into the struggle between humans and animals in *Animal Farm* is part of this crossing-over. See his Preface to the Ukrainian Edition of *Animal Farm—The Collected Essays, Journalism and Letters of George Orwell,* Vol. 3, eds., Sonia Orwell and Ian Angus (New York: Harcourt, Brace & World, 1968), pp. 402-406.

In "dwelling" the wound of ruination means that a "new figure" has been cut, one that works against the defense systems fabricating well-established identities and politics. "Cutting the quick" begins with reference to Franz Kafka's "In the Penal Colony" [*The Complete Stories*, ed. Nahum N. Glatzer (New York: Schocken Books, 1971)], and doubles the effect of cutting. A new figure is drawn from the defense systems and the defense systems themselves cut into this new figure. But inscribed and wounded bodies decipher their inscriptions in the same manner as the prisoners of the world's penal colonies.

The great systems are written on us. We feel them and their codes are deeply written in our hearts and revealed on our faces. Nietzsche and Kafka have written on revenge, but they warn that the deeper our inscriptions the more we like what they say—"The condemned man especially seemed struck with the notion that some great change was impending. What had happened to him was now going to happen to the officer. Perhaps even to the very end. Apparently the foreign explorer had given the order for it. So this was revenge. Although he himself had not suffered to the end, he was to be revenged to the end. A broad, silent grin now appeared on his face and stayed there all the rest of the time"—p. 163. The officer (say, Hitler) and the prisoner (say, Rabbi Ginsburg) are well-inscribed bodies and as such they believe in transcendental warrants. That is easier than tearing open the wounds in acts of substitution that rewrite the inscriptions.

"Second wind" tells a tale, partly autobiographical but also "fictional." To tell the "truth" is to cut too deeply, like the apparatus of Kafka's penal colony (see "Exile"). A fictional autobiography does not keep the reader from wandering with a less than sharply cut figure. The figure of this tale is a photographer who became a philosopher in search of the truth. The turn back to photography came with the turn to those outside the great texts of philosophy. Text, imaging, and the outsider seem to come together against the idolatry of "truth" and essences—see my "Easy Becoming Uneasy Images" and *Thinking With Pictures* (New Orleans: Art Review Press, 1990).

"You never get enough if you're good" reiterates the motivational system of truth/essence, attempting thereby to *show* the price exacted by that system (increasing abstractness and an ever-growing sense of self-importance) and how this extraction of debt is the mechanism which keeps us from everything outside. The apparatus of truth is, in other words, an isolating machine fed on bodies of knowledge (its own feeders). Such an apparatus is set against the very possibility of discourse—"discourse is not the majestically unfolding manifestation of a thinking, knowing, speaking subject, but, on the contrary, a totality, in which the dispersion of the subject and his discontinuity with himself may be determined. It is a space of exteriority in which a network of distinct sites is deployed" [Michel Foucault, *The Archaeology of Knowledge*, trans. A. M. Sheridan Smith (New York: Pantheon Books, 1972), p. 55]. In this kind of discourse, my two sites are images, photographic and otherwise, and philosophy. In this multivocal and intensely imaging discourse, one simply cannot be something—idolatry and the uni-dimensional site of monologue "go together." Here we might cite Leo Bersani, the outsider, who wrote of Freudian discourse: "Like the works of art which I have mentioned, the Freudian text is an exercise in discursive power which subversively points to the impossibility of its claims to power-generating knowledge. Freud's work is philosophy—or indeed any 'serious' cultural discourse—performing the reasons for its own radical frivolity"— *The Freudian Body: Psychoanalysis and Art* (New York: Columbia University Press, 1986), pp. 102-103).

"Working" takes anti-bodies of knowledge and their factories beyond the automation of the production of truth and essences—see my review of Richard Shaffer's art, "Anti-Bodies of Knowledge," *The New Orleans Art Review*, VII/3 (February/March 1989): 24-25. Working departs from the state and its isolating, reductive machines, especially those artificial breathing/punctuation devices.

"Perfect reproduction: eternal recurrence of the same no longer a riddle" reverses the customary sense of "common." It extends the discussion of isolating, reductive machines—the eternal recurrence of the same—by connecting Marx's notion of "dead labor" with such machines. The self-assured identity of the isolated "I" is precisely its loss of "common sense," the sense which is shared in the world of imaging, and the gain of revenge. Matters of passion and the heart are refined and converted by the reductive machinery of automation into logic and rationality. Listen to what Camus says of Sade and the state mechanisms of imprisonment: "The history and the tragedy of our times really begin with him [Sade]. He only believed that a society founded on freedom of crime must coincide with freedom of morals, as though servitude had its limits. Our times have limited themselves to blending, in a curious manner, his dream of a universal republic and his technique of degradation. Finally, what he hated most, legal murder, has availed itself of the discoveries that he wanted to put to the service of instinctive murder. Crime, which he wanted to be the exotic and delicious fruit of unbridled vice, is no more today than the dismal habit of a police-controlled morality"—*The Rebel*, p. 47.

The state inscribed itself deeply on Sade, who liked it so much that he called out to his torturers to make yet one more effort. Sadism is the terrifying image of the state become personal. See Marquis de Sade, *Juliette*, trans. Austryn Wainhouse (New York: Grove, 1968), pp. 771-72, where Sade has The Holy Father say: "the most useful crimes are without doubt those which most disrupt, such as the refusal to propagate and destruction; all the others are petty mischief, they are less even than that, or rather only those two merit the name of crime. . . . The existence of murderers is as necessary as that bane [war]; but for them, all would be disturbed in the order of things. It is therefore absurd to blame or punish them, more ridiculous still to fret over the natural inclinations which lead us to commit this act in spite of ourselves, for never will too many or enough murders be committed on earth, considering the burning thirst Nature has for them. . . . 'tis atrocity, 'tis scope she [Nature] wants in crimes; the more our destroying is of a broad and atrocious kind, the more agreeable it is to her."

Police-controlled morality is immorality made legal, and it is this positivism that construes everything untypical, alive, creative, common and plural a sin against the perfect reproductions of state-sponsored subjects. These subjects, or better, statoids, are the "profound" ones, the ones who can only expand vertically but never across to others different yet in common. The problem of what Lyotard calls the "differend" does not exist for the deep ones. They are also what Alan Rosenberg and Paul Marcus call "desk killers"—"The Holocaust as a Test of Philosophy" in *Echoes from the Holocaust.*

"J'accuse"—I accuse the idealists, the deep epistemology of forgetfulness, not of Being but of their role in ruining beings. Knowledge has always needed a leader, a central control unit directing the placement and use of its bodies. Two of Heidegger texts lay in the background of "J'accuse"— actually one text and one "withdrawn" comment: "Die Selbstbehauptung der deutschen Universität" and one of the few references Heidegger ever made to the Holocaust, a remark Heidegger made in his second Bremen lecture of 1949. The latter reads: "Agriculture is now a motorized food industry: in its essence it is the same thing as the manufacture of corpses in gas chambers, the same thing as blockades and the reduction of region to hunger, the same as the manufacture of hydrogen bombs"—as quoted in *Martin Heidegger and National Socialism*, p. xxx. For reasons of consistency and the preservation of his philosophical project, Heidegger withdrew this remark from the published version of this lecture—"Die Frage nach der Tecknik" (1955). I have explained the reasons for this "withdrawal" in "Why Heidegger Wasn't Shocked By The Holocaust." Here, however, it is only necessary to place this "withdrawn" in the context of what Heidegger's "Rectoral Address" says about the university and its leadership: "The very questionableness of Being forces the people to work and fight and forces it into its state [Staat], to which the professions belong. The three bonds—by the people, *to* the destiny of the state, *in* spiritual mission—are *equally primordial* to the German essence. The three services that arise from it—Labor Service, Military Service, and Knowledge Service—are equally necessary and of equal rank"—as quoted in *Martin Heidegger and National Socialism*, p. 11.

Philippe Lacoue-Labarthe [*Typography: Mimesis, Philosophy, Politics* (Cambridge: Harvard University Press, 1989), Chapter 6] is right when he argues that Heidegger's political engagement resumes the question of Being in the Greek sense (as Heidegger understood it). But Lacoue-Labarthe understates the "decisiveness" of Heidegger's thought when he says, "Let the error, or rather the *fault*, of Heidegger be what it may; I persist in believing that it removes absolutely nothing from the 'greatness' of his thought, that is to say, from its character—today for us—as decisive. A thought can be less than infallible and remain, as we say, 'impossible to avoid.' Its very infallibility, furthermore, gives us to think. This is why I persist in believing that it is also this thought itself that poses to us, out of its weakness, as out of its most extreme advances, the question of politics"—pp. 269-270. Yes, but it is more than the question of politics; it is also the complicity of philosophy with the state, the very statoid character of academic professions fortressed by defense systems. If I have learned anything from Heidegger, it is that philosophy cannot speak with transcendental warrants unless it is willing to practice "desk killing." This is exactly what Heidegger was willing to do for the sake of his project for the destruction of Western ontology and the question of Being by withdrawing his 1949 Bremen lecture remark on the Holocaust. J'accuse!

"A nietzschean tale" and "why the rational is not real" attempt to rescue Freud and Nietzsche, two thinkers the statoids are now trying to assimilate into their defensive systems. Why? Because both opened wounds that the state wants closed.

But thinking, crossing-over and connecting, keeps these wounds open—the stones still weep beneath the frames of knowledge placed over them. In other words, Freud and Nietzsche—and many others as well—are stories which "refuse any definitive ending." This refusal of endings, always against the projects of the desk killers, is the focus of "a grammatical note." The subject "man" is a patriarchal set-up—a beginning (privilege), middle, and end. The collaborator is male, the privileged subject of the patriarchal subject, the signifying power that speaks the set-up as his own. Which is why maids, to mention just one type of exclusion, never say anything when they clean-up after the events of truth.

There is a passage in Roland Barthes [*Camera Lucida: Reflections on Photography*, trans. Richard Howard (New York: Hill and Wang, 1982)] that "touches" my attempt to think with pictures: "For the noeme 'That-has-been' was possible only on the day when a scientific circumstance (the discovery that silver halogens were sensitive to light) made it possible to recover and print directly the luminous rays emitted by a variously lighted object. The photograph is literally an emanation of the referent. From the real body, which was there, proceed radiations which ultimately touch me, who am here; the duration of the transmission is insignificant; the photograph of the missing being, as Sontag says, will touch me like the delayed rays of a star. A sort of umbilical cord links the body of the photographed thing to my gaze: light, though impalpable, is here a carnal medium, skin I share with anyone who has been photographed"—pp. 80-81. Thus, "drawing on Barthes the semiographist" is an emanation that comes from combined images.

Anselm Kiefer's *Wege der Weltweisheit: Die Herrmanns-Schlacht* can be seen in the catalog of Kiefer's 1987-89 exhibition in Chicago, Philadelphia, Los Angeles, and New York—Mark Rosenthal, *Anselm Kiefer* (Philadephia: Philadelphia Museum of Art, 1987), p. 52. Rosenthal's interpretative essay on Kiefer's work is extremely sensitive to Kiefer's suspicion of all unbound transcendence. See also John C. Gilmour, *Fire on the Earth: Anselm Kiefer and the Postmodern World* (Philadelphia: Temple University Press, 1990).

"Undoing the imaginary" tells of my confrontation with Hegel, indirectly by way of his many "representatives" and directly by subversive readings of his texts. When I first read Hegel, I was indeed attempting to avoid the exclusions which Hegel disguised in his early writings as the triumph of Christianity [*Early Theological Writings*, trans. T. M. Knox (Philadelphia: University of Pennsylvania Press, 1971), Section I "The Positivity of the Christian Religion"]—a "triumph" which I believe is the foundation of the Hegelian "system" of thought. As I began to see that this "triumph" is neither spiritual nor conceptual, as I was becoming jew, I also began to see that the intended and stated goal of Hegel's texts is not the same as their movement as language. The very great scope of Hegel's writings lets too many things in, too many referents touching and displacing their intended goal. It is not Language but rather languages that will not do what Hegel wants them to do; languages are not the master (Language) that comes to itself through the conflict of its separation from itself in a world of fleshy carriers of the universal.

Consider what is necessary for the plausibility of this statement: "The national spirits, which become conscious of their being in the shape of some particular animal, coalesce into one single spirit. Thus it is that the separate artistically beautiful national spirits combine to form a Pantheon, the element and habitation of which is Language"—*Phenomenology of Spirit*, trans. J. B. Baille (London: George Allen & Unwin, 1964), p. 731. My experience with faces taught me that "particular animals" are materially and spiritually different, and that only some of these faces imaged within the standardized materials of the photographic industry. There are neither material nor spiritual substrates. Either experience teaches this or one simply stays within the defensive system that forms its members into various manifestations of "beautiful national spirits." But note that Hegel refers to a "Pantheon" which has language as its element and habitation. Pan's imaging is polyvalent. Not only does he survive (in part, in the devil of Christendom), his son Silenus became a companion of Dionysus. So, Pantheons come and go with the imagings of languages. No matter how many times you get sent back to school and the One, languages undo the Pantheons set up as graven images.

Is it needless to say that today much, perhaps our continued existence, depends on readings of Hegel? In "Violence and Metaphysics" Derrida says: "Philosophical language belongs to a system of language(s). Thereby, its nonspeculative ancestry always brings a certain equivocality into speculation. Since this equivocality is original and irreducible, perhaps philosophy must adopt it, think it and be thought in it, must accommodate duplicity and difference within speculation, within the very purity of philosophical meaning. No one, it seems to us, has attempted this more profoundly than Hegel"—*Writing and Difference*, p. 113.

"Normalcy" struggles with what could be called the "Hegelianizing" of the Holocaust. Monuments, required courses, very careful documentation, systematization, conferences, novels, films, etc.—and nothing changes in the still desperate hope that History is still moving towards its End. And all of this as the mutant faces image in their various ways.

"Repetition compulsion" refers to the industrial anti-work machine, which is also an indifference-producing machine. This is "business as usual." I have dealt with some of the consequences of this machinery that relate to the task of responding to the Holocaust in "Improprietary Thinking: No More Ours or Theirs," *Contemporary Philosophy*, XII/12 (November/December 1989).

"America the beautiful" connects the United States, its history and present myths, with the codes of the privileged subject's ascetic consumption in "facet two, spiritual consumption."

Indifference—objectivity, mirror imaging, self-assured identity— kills. "Mirror imaging" connects this murdering with the process of engendering, or the set-up of the patriarchal system of male privileging and its subsequent creation of fundamental ontologies.

"Dead-Ins?" does not pose a rhetorical question. The reader must decide the question of not only these texts, but the ones she will write tomorrow. Crinkum-Crankum, or, perhaps, you will be able to put me back into the reiterating flow of Being. I have been sent back, placed there, many times, but, so far, escaped each time. How? By "only" being a substitution among many others.

bibliography

ADORNO, Theodor W. *Negative Dialectics*, trans. E. B. Ashton (New York: The Seabury Press, 1973).

AMÉRY, Jean. *At the Mind's Limit: Contemplations By a Survivor On Auschwitz and Its Realities*, trans. Sidney Rosenfeld and Stella P. Rosenfeld (New York: Schocken Books, 1986).

AMÉRY, Jean. "On the Necessity and Impossibility of Being a Jew," *New German Critique*, 20 (Spring/Summer 1980): 15-29.

ARAD, Yitzhak, GUTMAN, Yisrael, MARGALIOT, Abraham, eds. *Documents on the Holocaust* (Jerusalem: Yad Vashem, 1981).

ARENDT, Hannah. *The Human Condition* (Chicago: University of Chicago Press, 1958).

ARENDT, Hannah. *The Life of the Mind*, 2 volumes (New York: Harcourt Brace Jovanovich, 1978).

ARENDT, Hannah. *The Origins of Totalitarianism* (New York: Harcourt, Brace & World, 1966).

BAKAN, David. *Disease, Pain, & Sacrifice: Toward a Psychology of Suffering* (Boston: Beacon Press, 1968).

BAKAN, David. *The Duality of Human Existence: Isolation and Communion in Western Man* (Boston: Beacon Press, 1966).

BARTHES, Roland. *Camera Lucida: Reflections on Photography*, trans. Richard Howard (New York: Hill and Wang, 1982).

BARTHES, Roland. *The Responsibility of Forms*, trans. Richard Howard (New York: Hill and Wang, 1985).

BARTHES, Roland. *The Rustle of Language*, trans. Richard Howard (New York: Hill and Wang, 1986).

BATAILLE, Georges. *Eroticism: Death & Sensuality*, trans. Mary Dalwood (San Francisco: City Lights Books, 1986).

BATAILLE, Georges. *Inner Experience*, trans. Leslie Anne Boldt (New York: State University of New York Press, 1988).

BAUER, Yehuda. *The Holocaust in Historical Perspective* (Seattle: University of Washington Press, 1978).

BAUDRILLARD, Jean. *America*, trans. Chris Turner (London: Verso, 1988).

BAUDRILLARD, Jean. *The Evil Demon of Images*, trans. Paul Patton and Paul Foss (Sydney: The Power Institute of Fine Arts, 1988).

202

BAUDRILLARD, Jean. *Selected Writings*, ed. Mark Poster (Stanford: Stanford University Press, 1988).

BAUDRILLARD, Jean. *The Evil Demon of Images*, trans. Paul Patton and Paul Foss (Sydney: The Power Institute of Fine Arts, 1988).

BAUMAN, Zygmunt. *Modernity and the Holocaust* (Ithaca: Cornell University Press, 1989).

BENJAMIN, Walter. *Illuminations: Essays and Reflections*, trans. Harry Zohn (New York: Harcourt, Brace & World, 1968).

BERGER, John X. and RICHON, Olivier. *Other Than Itself: Writing Photography* (Manchester: Cornerhouse Publications, 1989).

BERGSON, Henri. *Matter and Memory*, trans. N. M. Paul and W. S. Palmer (New York: Zone Books, 1988).

BERSANI, Leo. *The Freudian Body: Psychoanalysis and Art* (New York: Columbia University Press, 1986).

BETTELHEIM, Bruno. *Surviving and Other Essays* (New York: Alfred A. Knopf, 1979).

BLANCHOT, Maurice. *The Step Not Beyond*, trans. Lycette Nelson (Albany: State University of New York Press, 1992).

BLANCHOT, Maurice. *The Writing of the Disaster* (Lincoln: University of Nebraska Press, 1986).

BLOCH, Ernst. *Atheism in Christianity: The Religion of the Exodus and the Kingdom*, trans. J. T. Swann (New York: Herder and Herder, 1972).

BORKIN, Joseph. *The Crime and Punishment of I. G. Farben* (New York: The Free Press, 1978).

BROPHY, Brigid. *Black Ship to Hell* (New York: Harcourt, Brace & World, 1962).

BURGIN, Victor, ed. *Thinking photography* (London: Macmillan Education Ltd, 1990).

CAMUS, Albert. *The Myth of Sisyphus and Other Essays*, trans. Justin O'Brien (New York: Vintage Books, 1991).

CAMUS, Albert. *The Plague*, trans. Stuart Gilbert (New York: Modern Library, 1948).

CAMUS, Albert. *L'homme révolté* (Paris: Éditions Gallimard, 1951). *The Rebel*, trans. Anthony Bower (New York: Vintage Books, 1956).

CELAN, Paul. *Gesammelte Werke*, 5 volumes, eds. Beda Allemann and Stephan Reichert (Frankfurt am Main: Suhrkamp, 1986).

COHEN, Arthur A. *The Tremendum: A Theological Interpretation of the Holocaust* (New York: Crossroad, 1981).

COLIN, Amy. *Paul Celan: Holograms of Darkness* (Bloomington: Indiana University Press, 1991)

Concentration Camp Dachau 1933-1945 (Brussels: Comité International de Dachau, 1978).

DAVIDSON, Arnold, ed. "Symposium on Heidegger and Nazism," *Critical Inquiry*, 15/2 (Winter 1989).

DELBO, Charlotte. *None Of Us Will Return*, trans. John Githens (Boston: Beacon Press, 1978).

DELEUZE, Gilles, and GUATTARI, Félix. *Anti-Oedipus: Capitalism and Schizophrenia*, trans. Robert Hurley, Mark Seem, and Helen R. Lane (New York: The Viking Press, 1977).

DERRIDA, Jacques. *De l'esprit* (Paris: Editions Galilée, 1987).

DERRIDA, Jacques. *Glas*, trans. John P. Leavey and Richard Rand (Lincoln: University of Nebraska Press, 1986).

DERRIDA, Jacques. *Positions* (Paris: Les Éditions de Minuit, 1972).

DERRIDA, Jacques. *Writing and Difference*, trans. Alan Bass (Chicago: University of Chicago Press, 1978).

DEWEY, John. *The Quest for Certainty: A Study of the Relation of Knowledge and Action* (New York: Minton, Balch & Company, 1929).

DEWEY, John. *Reconstruction in Philosophy* (Boston: Beacon Press, 1948).

FACKENHEIM, Emil L. *Encounters between Judaism and Modern Philosophy* (New York: Schocken Books, 1980).

FACKENHEIM, Emil L. *God's Presence in History* (New York: Harper & Row, 1972).

FLEISCHNER, Eva, ed. *Auschwitz: Beginning of a New Era?* (New York: KTAV, 1977).

FOSTER, Hal, ed. *The Anti-Aesthetic: Essays on Postmodern Culture* (Port Townsend: Bay Press, 1983).

FÓTI, Véronique M. *Heidegger and the Poets: Poiesis/Sophia/Techne* (New Jersey: Humanities Press, 1992).

FOUCAULT, Michel. *Discipline and Punish: The Birth of the Prison*, trans. A. M. Sheridan (New York: Pantheon, 1978).

FOUCAULT, Michel. *Madness and Civilization*, trans. Richard Howard (New York: Vintage Books, 1973).

FOUCAULT, Michel. *Power/Knowledge: Selected Interviews & Other Writings 1972-1977*, ed. Colin Gordon (New York: Pantheon Books, 1980).

FOUCAULT, Michel. *The Archaeology of Knowledge*, trans. A. M. Sheridan Smith (New York: Pantheon Books, 1972).

FOUCAULT, Michel. *The Birth of the Clinic*, trans. A. M. Sheridan (New York: Vintage Books, 1975).

FOUCAULT, Michel. *The Order of Things*, trans. A. M. Sheridan (New York: Vintage Books, 1973).

FRASER, Nancy and NICHOLSON, Linda J. "Social Criticism without Philosophy: An Encounter between Feminism and Postmodernism," *Feminism/Postmodernism*, ed. Linda J. Nicholson (New York: Routledge, 1990).

FREUD, Sigmund. *Die Traumdeutung* (Frankfurt am Main: Fischer Taschenbuch, 1972).

FREUD, Sigmund. "The 'Uncanny'," *Collected Papers*, Vol. 4 (New York: Basic Books, 1959).

FREUD, Sigmund. *Moses and Monotheism*, trans. Katherine Jones (New York: Alfred A. Knopf, 1949).

FRIEDLÄNDER, Saul. *Reflections of Nazism: An Essay on Kitsch and Death*, trans. Thomas Weyr (New York: Harper & Row, 1984).

GADAMER, Hans-Georg. *Dialogue and Dialectic: Eight Hermeneutical Studies on Plato*, trans. P. Christopher Smith (New Haven: Yale University Press, 1980).

GASCHÉ, Rodolphe. *The Tain of the Mirror* (Cambridge: Harvard University Press, 1986).

GASS, William. "The Origin of Extermination in the Imagination," *The Philosophical Forum*, XVI/1-2 (Fall-Winter 1984-85): 19-32.

GENDLIN, Eugene. *Let Your Body Interpret Your Dreams* (Wilmette: Chiron Publications, 1986).

GENET, Jean. *Funeral Rites*, trans. Bernard Frechtman (New York: Grove Press, 1969).

GENET, Jean. *Miracle of the Rose*, trans. Bernard Frechtman (New York: Grove Press, 1966).

GILMOUR, John C. *Fire on the Earth: Anselm Kiefer and the Postmodern World* (Philadelphia: Temple University Press, 1990).

GOLDMANN, Lucien. *The Philosophy of the Enlightenment: The Christian Burgess and the Enlightenment*, trans. Henry Maas (Cambridge: The MIT Press, 1973).

HABERMAS, Jürgen. *Eine Art Schadensabwickung* (Frankfurt am Main: Suhrkamp, 1987).

HARAWAY, Donna J. *Simians, Cyborgs, and Women: The Reinvention of Nature* (New York: Routledge, 1991).

HARRIS, Thomas. *The Silence of the Lambs* (New York: St. Martin's Press, 1988).

HAYES, Peter. *Industry and Ideology: IG Farben in the Nazi Era* (Cambridge: Cambridge University Press, 1989).

HAYES, Peter, ed. *Lessons and Legacies: The Meaning of the Holocaust in a Changing World*, (Evanston: Northwestern University Press, 1991).

HEGEL, G. W. F. *Early Theological Writings*, trans. T. M. Knox (Philadelphia: University of Pennsylvania Press, 1971).

HEGEL, G. W. F. *Lectures on the Philosophy of World History: Introduction*, trans. H. B. Nisbet (New York: Cambridge University Press, 1975).

HEGEL, G. W. F. *Phänomenologie des Geistes* (Hamburg: Felix Meiner, 1952). Phenomenology of Spirit, trans. J. B. Baille (London: George Allen & Unwin, 1964).

HEGEL, G. W. F. *Wissenschaft der Logik,* 2 volumes (Frankfurt am Main: Suhrkamp, 1969).

HEIDEGGER, Martin. *Erläuterungen zu Hölderlins Dichtung* (Frankfurt am Main: Klostermann, 1971).

HEIDEGGER, Martin. *Nietzsche,* 2 volumes, (Stuttgart: Neske, 1961).

HEIDEGGER, Martin. *The End of Philosophy,* trans. Joan Stambaugh (New York: Harper & Row, 1973).

HEIDEGGER, Martin. *Sein und Zeit,* 11th Edition (Tübingen: Niemeyer, 1967); *Being and Time,* trans. John Macquarrie and Edward Robinson (New York, Harper & Row, 1962).

HEIDEGGER, Martin. *Unterwegs zur Sprache* (Tübingen: Neske, 1971).

HEIDEGGER, Martin. *Was Heisst Denken?* (Tübingen: Niemeter, 1971); *What Is Called Thinking?,* trans. Fred D. Wieck and J. Glenn Gray (New York: Harper & Row, 1968).

HEIDEGGER, Martin. *What is a Thing?,* trans. W. B. Barton, Jr. and Vera Deutsch (Chicago: Henry Regnery, 1970).

HILBERG, Raul. *The Destruction of the European Jews* (New York: Harper & Row, 1979).

HOMER. *The Iliad,* trans. Richard Lattimore (Chicago: The University of Chicago Press, 1951).

HOMER. *The Odyssey,* trans. Richard Lattimore (New York: Harper & Row, 1967).

HORKHEIMER, Max. *Critique of Instrumental Reason,* trans. J. O'Connell (New York: The Seabury Press, 1974).

HORKHEIMER, Max and ADORNO, Theodor W. *Dialectic of Enlightenment,* trans. John Cumming (New York: The Seabury Press, 1972).

HORKHEIMER, Max. *Eclipse of Reason* (New York: The Seabury Press, 1974).

HORKHEIMER, Max. *Dawn & Decline: Notes 1926-1931 & 1950-1969,* trans. Michael Shaw (New York: The Seabury Press, 1978).

HUYSSEN, Andreas. "The Politics of Identification: 'Holocaust' and West German Drama," *New German Critique,* 19 (Winter 1980): 117-136.

JASPERS, Karl. *Man in the Modern Age,* trans. Eden and Cedar Paul (New York: Anchor Books, 1957).

KAFKA, Franz. *The Complete Stories,* ed. Nahum N. Glatzer (New York: Schocken Books, 1971).

KANT, Immanuel. *Kritik der Reinen Vernunft* (Hamburg: Felix Meiner, 1956).

KANT, Immanuel. *Kritik der Urteilskraft* (Frankfurt am Main: Suhrkamp, 1978).

KAUFMANN, Walter. *Without Guilt and Justice: From Decidophobia to Autonomy* (New York: Peter H. Wyden, 1973).

KOGON, Eugen. *The Theory and Practice of Hell*, trans. Heinz Norden (New York: Berkley Books, 1980).

KOHN, Hans. *The Mind of Germany: The Education of a Nation* (New York: Charles Scribner's Sons, 1960).

KRISTEVA, Julia. *Powers of Horror: An Essay on Abjection*, trans. Leon S. Roudiez (New York: Columbia University Press, 1982).

KLOSSOWSKI, Pierre. *Sade My Neighbor*, trans. Alphonso Lingis (Evanston: Northwestern University Press, 1991).

LACAN, Jacques. *Écrits* (Paris: Éditions du Seuil, 1966).

LACOUE-LABARTHE, Philippe. *Heidegger, Art and Politics: The Fiction of the Political*, trans. Chris Turner (Cambridge: Basil Blackwell, 1990).

LACOUE-LABARTHE, Philippe. *Typography: Mimesis, Philosophy, Politics* (Cambridge: Harvard University Press, 1989).

LAING, R. D. *Self and Others* (New York: Pantheon Books, 1961).

LANG, Berel. "The Concept of Genocide," *The Philosophical Forum*, XVI/ 1-2 (Fall-Winter 1984-85): 1-18.

LANGER, Lawrence L. *The Age of Atrocity: Death in Modern Literature* (Boston: Beacon Press, 1978).

LEVI, Primo. *If This is a Man: Remembering Auschwitz* (New York: Summit Books, 1985).

LEVI, Primo. *The Drowned and the Saved*, trans. Raymond Rosenthal (New York: Summit Books, 1986).

LEVINAS, Emmanuel. *Collected Philosophical Papers*, trans. Alphonso Lingis (Dordrecht: Martinus Nijhoff, 1987).

LEVINAS, Emmanuel. *Ethics and Infinity: Conversations with Philippe Nemo*, trans. Richard A. Cohen (Pittsburgh: Duquesne University Press, 1985).

LEVINAS, Emmanuel. *Otherwise Than Being or Beyond Essence*, trans. Alphonso Lingis (The Hague: Martinus Nijhoff, 1981).

LEVINAS, Emmanuel. *Time and the Other*, trans. Richard A. Cohen (Pittsburgh: Duquesne University Press, 1987).

LÉVI-STRAUSS, Claude. *The Raw and the Cooked: Introduction to a Science of Mythology*, Vol. I, trans. John and Doreen Weightman (New York: Harper & Row, 1969).

LYOTARD, Jean-François. *Heidegger and "the jews,"* trans. Andreas Michel and Mark Roberts (Minneapolis: University of Minnesota Press, 1990).

LYOTARD, Jean-François. *Libidinal Economy*, trans. Iain Hamilton Grant (Bloomington: Indiana University Press, 1993).

LYOTARD, Jean-François. *The Differend: Phrases in Dispute*, trans. Georges Van Den Abbeele (Minneapolis: University of Minnesota Press, 1988).

LYOTARD, Jean-François. *The Postmodern Condition: A Report on Knowledge*, trans. Geoff Bennington and Brian Massumi (Minneapolis: University of Minnesota Press, 1984).

MARX, Karl. *Capital*, 3 volumes, trans. Samuel Moore and Edward Aveling (New York: International Publishers, 1967).

MARX, Karl. *Grundrisse: Foundations of the Critique of Political Economy*, trans. Martin Nicolaus (New York: Vintage Books, 1973).

MARX, Karl/ENGELS, Frederick. *Collected Works*, Volumes 3 and 4 (New York: International Publishers, 1975).

MENDELSOHN, John, ed. *The Holocaust: Selected Documents in Eighteen Volumes* (New York: Garland Publishing, 1982).

MERLEAU-PONTY, Maurice. *The Prose of the World*, trans. John O'Neill (Evanston: Northwestern University Press, 1973).

MERLEAU-PONTY, Maurice. *The Visible and the Invisible*, trans. Alphonso Lingis (Evanston: Northwestern University Press, 1968).

MILLER, Frank. *Batman: The Drak Knight Returns* (New York: DC Comics, 1986).

MOSSE, George L. *Nazi Culture* (New York: Schocken Books, 1981).

NESKE, Günther and KETTERING, Emil. *Martin Heidegger and National Socialism*, trans. Lisa Harries and Joachim Neugroschel (New York: Paragon House, 1990).

NEUGROSCHEL, Joachim, ed. and trans. *The Shtetl: A Creative Anthology of Jewish Life in Eastern Europe* (New York: Richard Marek, 1979).

NIETZSCHE, Friedrich. *Also sprach Zarathustra* (Frankfurt am Main: Insel, 1979); *Thus Spoke Zarathustra*, trans. Walter Kaufmann (New York: Viking Penguin, 1966).

NIETZSCHE, Friedrich. *Jenseits von Gut und Böse* (Frankfurt am Main: Insel, 1984).

NIETZSCHE, Friedrich. *On the Genealogy of Morals/Ecce Homo*, trans. Walter Kaufmann (New York: Viking Penguin, 1969).

NIETZSCHE, Friedrich. *The Will To Power*, trans. Walter Kaufmann and R. J. Hollingdale (New York: Random House, 1967).

NIETZSCHE, Friedrich. *Twilight of the Idols/The Anti-Christ*, trans. R. J. Hollingdale (New York: Viking Penguin, 1968).

ORWELL, George. *The Collected Essays, Journalism and Letters*, 4 volumes, ed. Sonia Orwell and Ian Angus (New York: Harcourt, Brace & World, 1968).

POSTER, Mark, ed. *Jean Baudrillard: Selected Writings* (Stanford: Stanford University Press, 1988).

208

POSTONE, Moishe. "Anti-Semitism and National Socialism: Notes on the German Reaction to 'Holocaust'," *New German Critique*, 19 (Winter 1980): 97-115.

PLATO. *The Collected Dialogues*, eds., Edith Hamilton and Huntington Cairns (Princeton: Princeton University Press, 1961).

PYNCHON, Thomas. *Vineland* (Boston: Little, Brown and Company, 1990).

RABINBACH, Anson. "The Jewish Question in the German Question," *New German Critique: Special Issue on the Historikerstreit*, 44 (Spring/Summer 1988): 159-192.

RAULET, Gérard. "The Logic of Decomposition: German Poetry in the 1960s," *New German Critique*, 21 (Fall 1980): 81-112.

RÉMOND, René, et al., eds. *Paul Touvier et L'église* (Paris: Fayard, 1992).

RICOEUR, Paul. *The Symbolism of Evil*, trans. Emerson Buchanan (Boston: Beacon Press, 1969).

ROCKMORE, Tom and MARGOLIS, Joseph, eds. *The Heidegger Case: On Philosophy and Politics* (Philadelphia: Temple University Press, 1992).

RONELL, Avital. *The Telephone Book: Technology, Electric Speech* (Lincoln: University of Nebraska Press, 1989).

RORTY, Richard. *Contingency, irony, and solidarity* (New York: Cambridge University Press, 1989).

RORTY, Richard. *Essays on Heidegger and Others* (New York: Cambridge University Press, 1991).

ROSENBERG, Alan and MEYERS, Gerald E., eds. *Echoes from the Holocaust: Philosophical Reflections on a Dark Time* (Philadelphia: Temple University Press, 1988).

ROSENTHAL, Mark. *Anselm Kiefer* (Philadelphia: Philadelphia Museum of Art, 1987).

ROTENSTREICH, Nathan. "Can Evil Be Banal?," *The Philosophical Forum*, XVI/1-2 (Fall-Winter 1984-85): 50-62.

ROTENSTREICH, Nathan. *Tradition and Reality* (New York: Random House, 1972).

ROTH, John K. and BERENBAUM, Michael, eds. *Holocaust: Religious and Philosophical Implications* (New York: Paragon House, 1989).

RUBINSTEIN, Richard L. *The Cunning of History: The Holocaust and the American Future* (New York: Harper & Row, 1975).

RUBINSTEIN, Richard L. "The Unmastered Trauma: Interpreting the Holocaust," *Humanities in Society*, 2/4 (Fall 1979): 417-433.

RUETHER, Rosemary. *Faith and Fratricide: The Theological Roots of Anti-Semitism* (New York: Seabury Press, 1979).

SADE, Marquis de. *Juliette*, trans. Austryn Wainhouse (New York: Grove, 1968).

SARTRE, Jean-Paul. *Critique de la raison dialectique*, Vol. I (Paris: Gallimard, 1960).

SARTRE, Jean-Paul. *Saint Genet: Actor and Martyr*, trans. Bernard Frechtman (New York: Mentor Book, 1963).

SARTRE, Jean-Paul. *The Transcendence of the Ego: An Existential Theory of Consciousness*, trans. Forrest Williams and Robert Kirkpatrick (New York: The Noonday Press, 1957).

SCHÜRMANN, Reiner. *Heidegger on Being and Acting: From Principles to Anarchy*, trans. Christine-Marie Gros (Bloomington: Indiana University Press, 1987).

SILVERMAN, Hugh J., ed. *Questioning Foundations*, Vol. V of "Continental Philosophy" series (New York: Routledge, 1993).

SOPHOCLES. *Oedipus the King*, trans. Stephen Berg and Diskin Clay (New York: Oxford University Press, 1978).

SPEIGELMAN, Art. *Maus: A Survivor's Tale* (New York: Pantheon Books, 1986).

SULEIMAN, Susan Rubin, ed. *The Female Body in Western Culture* (Cambridge: Harvard University Press, 1986).

SZASZ, Thomas S. *The Manufacture of Madness: A Comparative Study of the Inquisition and the Mental Health Movement* (New York: Harper & Row, 1970).

The Black Book: The Nazi Crime Against the Jewish People (New York: Duell, Sloan and Pearce, 1946).

VATTIMO, Gianni. *The End of Modernity: Nihilism and Hermeneutics in Postmodern Culture*, trans. Jon R. Synder (Baltimore: John Hopkins University Press, 1988).

WALLIS, Brian, ed. *Art After Modernism: Rethinking Representation* (New York: The New Museum of Contemporary Art, 1984).

WATSON, James R. "Auschwitz and the Limits of Transcendence," Philosophy & Social Criticism, 18/2 (1992).

WATSON, James R. "Easy Becoming Uneasy Images: A Photogrammic Solarization of Caves," *Questioning Foundations*, ed. Hugh Silverman (New York: Routledge, 1993).

WATSON, James R. "Improprietary Thinking: No More Ours or Theirs," *Contemporary Philosophy*, XII/11 (1990).

WATSON, James R. "Richard Shaffer: Anti-Bodies of Knowledge," *New Orleans Art Review*, VII/3 (Feb/Mar 1989).

WATSON, James R. *Thinking With Pictures* (New Orleans: Art Review Press, 1990).

WATSON, James R. "Why Heidegger Was Not Shocked By The Holocaust," *History of European Ideas, 14/4 (1992)*.

WIESEL, Elie. *A Jew Today*, trans. Marion Wiesel (New York: Random House, 1978).

WIESEL, Elie. *One Generation After* (New York: Simon & Schuster, 1970).

WIESEL, Elie. *The Night Trilogy: Night, Dawn, and The Accident* (New York: The Noonday Press, 1987).

WIESEL, Elie. *Zalmen, or the Madness of God* (New York: Random House, 1974).

WIESENTHAL, Simon. *The Sunflower* (New York: Schocken Books, 1976).

WYSCHOGROD, Edith. *Spirit in Ashes: Hegel, Heidegger, and Man-Made Mass Death* (New York: Yale University Press, 1985).

YOUNG, James E. *Writing and Rewriting the Holocaust: Narrative and the Consequences of Interpretation* (Bloomington: Indiana University Press, 1988).

ZUR, Ofer. "The Love of Hating: The Psychology of Enmity," *History of European Ideas*, 13/4 (1991): 345-369.

index

VALUE INQUIRY BOOK SERIES

VIBS